THE COUNTRY DIARY BOOK OF

Creating a Wild Flower Garden

THE COUNTRY DIARY BOOK OF

Creating a Wild Flower Garden

—— Jonathan Andrews ——

Edited and with an Introduction by
Anthony Huxley

Bloomsbury Books
London

DEDICATION
To C, J and A
for their help and inspiration

First published in Great Britain 1986 by
Webb & Bower (Publishers) Limited
9 Colleton Crescent, Exeter, Devon EX2 4BY

in association with Michael Joseph Limited
27 Wright's Lane. London W8 5SL

First impression 1986
Second impression 1991
Third impression 1994

Designed by Malcolm Couch

Production by Nick Facer

This edition published 1994 by
Bloomsbury Books an imprint of
Godfrey Cave Associates
42 Bloomsbury Street, London WC1B 3QJ
under license from Michael Joseph Limited

ISBN 1–85471–401–5

The publishers would like to thank Rowena Stott,
Edith Holden's great-niece and the owner of the original work,
who has made the publication of this
book possible.

Printed and bound in Spain
★ ★ ★ ★ ★

Contents

Foreword

ANTHONY HUXLEY

Wild flowers, once so common as to be an essential part of everyday country life, have come increasingly into our consciousness and equally our conscience in recent years, as it becomes apparent how much of nature has disappeared – to buildings and roads, technological agriculture, forestry plantations and many another inroad. Weedkillers wipe out wild flowers in crops and field margins, and fertilisers put paid to them in grassland; drainage obliterates specialised damp habitats, and loss of woodland diminishes another whole gamut of species adapted to such haunts.

The destruction is horrifying in every country. In North America the prairies of the Middle West, and the badlands caused by their careless management half a century ago, have not a wild flower left in a country of which an early settler could write how 'the strawberries grew so thick that horses' fetlocks seemed covered in blood.' In all-too-small Britain, where acre-by-acre statistics are more easily counted, we have in the last 40 years destroyed 95% of our natural meadows, 80% of downland with its short sheep-grazed turf, 60% of lowland heaths, half our fens and marshes and half of our often ancient deciduous woods. Around 125,000 miles of hedgerow have gone too, many again very ancient, man-made certainly but acting as harbours of plants and other wildlife between crop fields and pastures where any other natural habitats may have been entirely removed.

With the plants that create these habitats disappear animals of every kind; the smaller, more attractive birds become fewer, while the most noticeable losses have been of butterflies and dragonflies, and to a lesser extent bees, all vulnerable both to loss of habitat and increased use of pesticides.

In face of these assaults on nature many people have turned to the possibility of making their gardens, at least in part, into miniature conservation areas. They grow plants which will encourage birds, insects and small mammals, and arrange their gardens so that there is much less disturbance than in the usual run of ornamental gardening.

In fact, many well known garden varieties which have been improved by man's selection and breeding can be used in this way; the Asiatic Buddleia is a good example, one of the best shrubs for attracting butterflies. But many wild gardeners prefer to grow only native species, and to encourage the less common ones is clearly an important aspect of conservation. In a wild garden plants which are normally treated as weeds are usually allowed to grow, but many wild species are very attractive in their own right.

This emphasis on wild plants is what this book is really about. It is illustrated with a selection of the wild flower paintings which first appeared in Edith Holden's celebrated *Country Diary of an Edwardian Lady*. Each of these beautifully recorded plants is accompanied by text which stresses the place of the plant in folklore, certain culinary uses if it has them, and its herbal or medicinal properties.

Folklore, and its darker side, witchcraft, open up a fascinating world which used to imbue the minds of country dwellers almost within living memory. The country names of plants, so intriguing in themselves – and really needing a dictionary to explain them – record the deep involvement of people with the plants around them; one can be sure that the more local names a plant has the more significant it was in folklore terms. Here only a selection of these quaint names can be included; those interested in a fuller record should go to Geoffrey Grigson's incomparable *An Englishman's Flora*.

It must be said that the herbal recommendations mentioned in these pages, for medicinal, tonic and occasionally cosmetic purposes, are sometimes based on real worth but perhaps more often only on tradition. The ancient Doctrine of Signatures is responsible for many of the latter – a belief that if a plant resembled an organ of the body, or in some cases a disease, it must have been designed by providence to cure ailments of that organ, or that disease. Once in a while coincidence made this true. A classic example is the willow, the quivering leaves of which suggested its herbal use, as an infusion of the bark, to cure the ague; and in the nineteenth century chemical investigation resulted in the isolation of salicin, which proved the key to acetylsalicylic acid or aspirin.

Plant constituents enter into over 40% of western pharmaceutical products, and our pharmacopoeias list some 400 plant sources. In the Third World, three-quarters of medical needs are met by herbal preparations and some 6,000 plants are involved. Increasingly, remedies for difficult conditions are being met by compounds isolated from plants as scientists examine tribal usage and screen new species; in many cases the complexity of plant compounds is beyond chemical synthesis.

However, a little knowledge being a dangerous thing, it should go without saying that ordinary people should not experiment with medications from poisonous plants like foxglove, nightshades and henbane. Remedies based on such plants – and there are many – must only be taken on medical advice in proper formulations. But herbal teas and infusions, for instance, for tonic or other purposes, can be made following recipes in herbal books.

When it comes to establishing wild plants in the garden the choice is very large. Most seedsmen now offer a limited range of wild flower seeds suitable for naturalising, and there are more extensive lists. In Britain the major specialist lists around 600 different kinds and offer many mixtures suitable for one condition or another – for instance woodland, hedgerows, damp places, seaside, and different types of soil. Others, suitable for making 'mini-meadows', contain both wild flowers and native grasses. Yet others provide plants specially to encourage butterflies, bees and birds, and among further possibilities are edible, spice and dye plants.

Brief cultural instructions are given in this book. In principle let us remember that most wild plants spread readily by their own simple methods; in many cases all one needs to do is follow nature's way and sow seeds when they would ripen in the wild. Light forking and raking over of soil to provide a good tilth – to use that old gardener's term for a well prepared seed bed – will help the seeds along, and when the young plants develop they can be transplanted where one wants.

It goes, I hope, without saying that in principle wild plants should never be dug up and transplanted; the only exceptions being from places where they are going to be destroyed by building or a new road, or from rubbish tips where sometimes remarkable assemblages of 'weeds' develop.

Once established many wild plants extend by overground runners or underground rhizomes, and annual kinds are usually lavish with seeds. Not all wild plants are weeds in garden terms, which usually means a well developed aggressiveness, but few are not equipped to spread and compete with neighbours. This is important to remember when planting, especially in suburbia where invasive roots like bindweed or masses of floating seeds like thistles will not be welcomed by neighbours – one might not wish to include all the plants pictured in the *Country Diary*!

The spreading capacity of wild plants also has a bearing on the amount of access wanted, and of annual tidying up that one may wish. A fully wild garden fills up with competing plants with the result that some will be overwhelmed. So if one is growing some plants for their own sake rather than an overall, uncurbed wild habitat, some 'gardening' is essential to curb the most vigorous kinds, ensure that treasures like small bulbs or rarities are not smothered, and see that shrubs and even trees are not strangled by fast-growing climbers. Let me emphasise that there is absolutely no need for a wild garden to be a wilderness.

Nor is there any reason why a garden partly or entirely devoted to wild plants, and designed to encourage wild life, should not be attractive. Many wild plants have as much beauty as highly bred garden varieties; there is often an airy charm in species which their garden cousins lack. Their comparative beauty is very much in the eye of the beholder.

One can have turf spangled with appropriate short flowers, areas of longer grass with taller flowers, borders of herbaceous plants, shrub areas, pools where native water-lovers are as decorative as many exotics, interspersed or backed with trees. Such plantings are possible even in quite small areas, and if desired more orthodox ornamental gardening can blend into a wild area imperceptibly. The long narrow town plot or 'suburban strip' is well shaped for such treatment – normal garden planting and control with a sitting-out place near the house and wilder areas at the further end. Such a combination could be said to give the gardener the best of two worlds.

None of these ideas, I am sure, was ever in Edith Holden's mind when she portrayed wild flowers or animals, nor when she produced the 'Nature Notes for 1906' which were later reproduced as *The Country Diary of an Edwardian Lady*. Although the countryside in England was increasingly encroached upon by industrial and dormitory towns, roads and railways, it was always thought of as something distinct, as a refuge for town dwellers to escape to; very much as something that was abundant enough in its manifestations of wood, meadow, down and marsh, to seem limitless, something the continuity of which was not a problem. The pattern of cultivation was very much as it had been for centuries, and the colourful weeds in crops were a part of that system.

Her Nature Notes show keen observation of plants and their ways, and of the animals which they provided food and homes for; and they also show a wide knowledge of nature poetry.

All this was to be expected from middle-class young ladies of most of the nineteenth century: it was habitual for them to be taught painting, and very often they went on primarily to depict flowers and landscapes. This leisure activity continued through the Victorian and Edwardian eras and up to the dream-shattering beginning of the first world war. Edith Holden, born in 1871, was in the mainstream of this tradition.

Unlike most such young ladies, she had a real aptitude for art, as is shown by her attending the Birmingham School of Art from the age of thirteen; when nineteen she had an oil painting accepted for the Royal Birmingham Society of Artists' exhibition. Her art training was among many fellow pupils who became well known book illustrators, and when twenty her art tutors suggested that she might study with Joseph Denovan Adam, a well known animal painter. By 1894 Edith was joining forces with her older sister Violet in their first ventures into book illustration; they did two together, and Edith eventually had seven further illustrated books to her credit, as well as contributing to many issues of *The Animals' Friend*, the magazine of the National Council for Animals' Welfare.

The 'Nature Notes for 1906' were compiled for the first full year of the Holdens move to Olton, near Birmingham (and now a suburb of it). It was her aim to record all the flowers and birds she found in this new area, nearer the town than the various houses where she had spent her childhood in the open country of north Warwickshire. Occasionally she comments on new plantings in the garden of their Olton house.

One feels fairly sure that Edith Holden expected her oil paintings to provide whatever immortality she may have hoped for. It is ironic that of about fifty she exhibited between 1890 and 1907, the whereabouts of none are known. Although she used some of the paintings in 'Nature Notes' as a basis for the calendars and illustrations in *The Animals' Friend*, this chapbook, a year's pastime in a period of leisure, was most certainly never thought of for publication as an entity in its own right.

Yet it has provided pleasure to many thousands of readers since its reactivation as *The Country Diary*, and one hopes that this further sampling of the flowers it portrays will now give encouragement to the very desirable possibilities of making wildlife gardens which will harbour the plants and animals she loved in an era of continuing inroads upon nature.

Portrait of Edith Holden
reproduced by kind permission of Esmond Holden

Author's Note

The inspiration for this present book comes directly from a long-standing interest in wild flowers fostered, initially, by my parent's love of the countryside of their native Devon, and from an increasing concern for the preservation of our inherited wildlife and natural flora.

Although not intended as such, originally, Edith Holden's Nature Notes acts as a powerful reminder of much that we have perhaps failed to preserve since the turn of the century. Of the many once common wild flowers which she mentioned I have featured those which can most readily be introduced into a planned wild flower garden.

Growing wild flowers is no more difficult than the growing of more familiar garden varieties. There is no special mystique attached to their cultivation, and there is also much to be gained from an appreciation of each plant's placc in mythology and the herbal practices of day's gone by. It is hoped, therefore, that this book will act as an introduction to the possibilities of growing our wild and beautiful natural flowers in your own garden.

Jonathan Andrews

The Wild Flower Season

Gentle Wood Sorrel in a woodland setting.

On the following pages the wild flowers have been included according to their flowering season – when they are at their best and will give greatest enjoyment in the wild flower garden. With a few exceptions, wild flowers in their natural habitats flower between early Spring and the Autumn. A 'season' which also applies to those which you have chosen for the garden, although the work involved in their preparation and cultivation will extend far beyond this flowering time.

For each of the plants simple cultural instructions are given regarding the best times for sowing, planting container-grown flowers and the most favourable garden situations. As most wild flowers featured very prominently in the lives of past generations, the legends surrounding each flower and its past herbal, medicinal and culinary uses are also covered together with some of the many intriguing local country names for each flower. The second part of this book deals with more general cultivation methods, the role of butterflies and bees during their own season on the wing and suggestions for planning your own wild flower garden.

January and February

During both January and February we can experience the coldest weather of the year and even in the mildest Winter there will be many days of unfavourable wind and rain.

However, during February the first wild flowers will appear. In the countryside, hedgerows will show the first vigorous growth of the Wild Arum, Stinging Nettles and Primroses and although in certain parts of the country the Snowdrop might well have come through during the previous month, in February both it and the Sweet Violet should be in bloom.

In the wild flower garden the weather may not be favourable for many tasks, but on the occasional good day as much preparation for the coming season should be attempted as possible. Unless the soil is too wet and compacted continue with general digging and the preparing of seed beds, ensuring that these are weed-free. Check also the progress of seeds sown either under glass at the end of last year or those which have been left outdoors for exposure to Winter frosts.

Sweet Violet

Viola odorata

March Violet, English Violet.

The Violet symbolises constancy, humility and modesty and was the symbol of Athens and, more recently, Rhode Island, Illinois and New Jersey.

Perfume from the plant has been used for centuries not only in cosmetics, but also in the preparation of 'sherbet' in the Middle East. In England the Violet was frequently used to carpet the floors of musty smelling churches and houses.

When Napoleon was banished to Elba his final parting words were to the effect that he would return with the Violets in the Spring. He actually re-entered the Tuileries on March 20th, in time with the flowers.

He had always given Violets to Josephine on their wedding anniversaries and his parting statement was taken up by his supporters who adopted the Violet as their secret symbol, and password.

The generic name comes from the Greek *ion* and the Latin *viola*. Due to its scented qualities and the associations with sexual love it was also adopted by the Greeks as the symbol of Aphrodite and her son Priapus. It frequently appears in old herbals as a cure for headaches, and as a mouthwash and gargle.

Viola odorata flowers earlier than the Dog Violet, *V. riviniana*, with the Sweet Violet blooming until May and the Dog Violet from May until as late as August.

The Sweet Violet is extremely high in Vitamin C and a dish called *vyolette* was once popular in England. For this the flowers were boiled and pressed, with additions of milk, rice flour and honey.

Sweet Violet

Sweet Violet

Perennial

Size:	Up to 5in (12.5cm)
Flowers:	February – April
Sowing:	Sow in cold frame or in trays of seed compost in late Summer. Over-winter in protected area and plant in flowering position in Spring. It is important to have as much rootstock and soil as possible when re-planting. Divide clumps in Autumn.
Position:	Well-drained soil, moist, with some acid content. Sun or partial shade.
Note:	The flowering of the Sweet Violet can be erratic and it will occasionally flower in Autumn as well as Spring.

In addition to being scentless the Dog Violet has much narrower leaves than the Sweet Violet, and while the flowers of Sweet Violet can be deep blue, lilac or even white the flowers of the Dog Violet are invariably clear blue.

Dog Violet

Dog Violet

Viola riviniana

Blue Mice, Cuckoo's Shoes, House Violet, Hypocrites, Shoes and Stockings, Snake Violet.

Very often considered to be the poor relation of the Sweet Violet, *Viola riviniana* is no less attractive a plant. But being scentless the prefix 'Dog' has been applied, as with other plants felt to be inferior in some way to their relations.

Gerard coined the now traditional English name for this scentless Violet in the sixteenth century when he translated the name directly from the Latin *Viola canina*.

Dog Violet

Perennial

Size:	Up to 6in (15cm)
Flowers:	Spring and Autumn
Sowing:	The Dog Violet requires Winter frosts and cold to break down seed husk. Plant seeds, if ripe, in March/April for Autumn flowering. Or, sow in trays of rich compost in late Summer and place outdoors, covered, during Winter. Plant out in Spring.
Position:	Rich, well-drained soil with partial shade.

Snowdrop

Galanthus nivalis

Blackbird Flower, Candlemas Bells, Death's Flower, Dingle Bell, Fair-Maids-of-February, Snow Piercer, White Gallant.

The Snowdrop is probably not a native plant to Britain and the name is likely to have been an anglicised version of the Swedish name *snödroppe*, and the German *schneeglöckchen*, a 'snow-bell'. Some think that it was introduced by monks during the fifteenth century and although it was certainly growing in England in Elizabethan times, Shakespeare makes no mention of it in his works and the name first appears about the time that Thomas Johnson published a revised edition of Gerard's *Herbal* in 1633. When writing of the previously named Early-Flowering Bulbous Violet he stated that 'some do call them … snowdrops'.

But surely one of the most vivid, descriptive names for this hardy little flower was 'snow-piercer' – *pierce-neige* in French – as the Snowdrop was one of the earliest flowers to appear each year, in even the severest of conditions. In certain parts of the country it can appear as early as New Year's Day.

The Snowdrop was a symbol of purity and young girls collected them for the decoration of churches prior to the ceremonies surrounding the Feast of Purification on Candlemas Day, 2nd February. Yet it was also considered unlucky for these same girls to pick the Snowdrop, particularly if the first spray was brought into the home, because a fatality would certainly occur; in many areas of the country the Snowdrop carried the name of 'Death's Flower'.

Fair-Maids-of-February

Size:	Up to 8in (20.5cm)
Flowers:	January – April
Sowing:	Snowdrops are best grown from bulbs which can remain in the soil for years. Plant 2 – 3in (5 – 7.5cm) deep in rich moist soil in late Summer for flowering the next Spring. Divide clumps if necessary and move after flowering before leaves die away.
Position:	Lawn edges, in grassy areas, in sun or partial shade.
Note:	The bulbs from Snowdrops grown indoors can be relocated in the garden after flowering.

March

March can be a most unpredictable month, from the point of view of the weather. In an ideal season it should be dry and not too cold nor yet too warm, but very often March is a month of extremes and certain to be windy at some stage. However, this wind can be something of a blessing as it can dry out the top soil quite adequately for future activities.

In even the poorest March weather Wood Anemones, Snowdrops, Daffodils and Primroses will be making an appearance in the wild, and now is the time that many of the seeds which were started during the previous year before the onset of Winter, will demand attention. Towards the end of the month, if the weather is mild and the soil dry enough, plant out those seedlings which are ready, into their planned flowering positions.

Although there are few seeds which can now be sown direct into open ground there are many which can be started under glass – such as the Primroses and Lesser Celandines – which will then be ready for planting out later in the year for flowering the following Spring.

Complete your ordering of seeds from seed merchants, for sowing in the coming months.

Common Gorse
or Whin

Gorse

Ulex europaeus

Fingers and Thumbs, French Fuzz, Hawth, Hoth, Honey Bottles, Pins and Needles.

Gorse does not spring very readily to mind as a true wild flower, but because of its use for hedging and the division of plots, and its place in folklore and tradition it is not to be dismissed from the 'wild flower garden'.

During March, hills and moorland are covered with the glorious yellow flowers of the Gorse. The Swedish botanist, Linnaeus, was believed to have fallen to his knees and praised God for the dramatic sight of Putney Heath ablaze with Gorse blossom.

The flowers cease in June. A traditional saying held that 'when gorse is out of bloom, kissing is out of fashion'. But by switching ones attention to *Ulex minor*, the dwarf gorse, which flowers well into the Autumn, one may safely remain in fashion.

Gorse was a popular fuel in the home and in various industries such as bakery and brick-making, before the advent of the coal industry. In Scotland the young shoots of gorse, or whin as it was called, were pounded down in *whinmills* and used as winter feed for cattle, and the bark of Gorse is still used today to dye certain tartan cloth.

A powerful plant against fairies and witches. In Ireland, where it was known as the 'Blessed Furze', and Wales, bunches of Gorse and Hawthorn were hung above the doors of the house on May Day to ward off evil influences.

Perennial

Size:	8 – 9ft (2.4 – 2.7m)
Flowers:	March – late June
Sowing:	Either sow seeds in prepared site in Spring, thinning out when larger, or sow into pots which can then be planted in growing position later in the year. Container-grown shrubs and nursery stock should be planted in Spring.
Position:	Ordinary or even poor soil if there is no lime present. A good hedging plant, but should not be moved from growing site once established.
Note:	Unlike Broom, can be clipped and pruned back quite hard in the Autumn.

Primrose

Primula vulgaris

Butter Rose, Darling of April, Easter Rose, Ladies of Spring, Lent Rose, May Flower.

A firm favourite among lovers of the countryside and eagerly sought as the first promise of Spring and the Summer to follow.

During a mild March in 1906 Edith found abundant quantities of Primrose in the surrounding fields. Regrettably, so too have generations of others, and over-picking of the plant has inevitably led to the Primrose becoming virtually extinct in many areas. The name comes from the Medieval Latin *prima rosa*, the first rose of the year. This allusion to the rose is reflected in many of the regional names for *Primula vulgaris*.

Disraeli stated that it was his favourite flower. After learning of this Queen Victoria included it with many of the bouquets she presented to him over the years, and she sent a wreath of the blooms to his funeral. The Primrose League and also the Tory Party took the flower as its symbol.

The healing properties of the Primrose have been appreciated for centuries. The Romans gathered them in order to fight off malarial fevers, and Culpeper advised a salve of the leaves for the healing of 'diverse wounds'. During the nineteenth century an ointment from the plant was applied to rid the face of freckles and tans, and an infusion made to cure coughs.

Perhaps one of the most curious of customs was that, in Germany, Primroses were believed to reveal the location of hidden treasure, and the flower was called the 'key flower', *schusselblume*.

Perennial	
Size:	4in (10cm)
Flowers:	March – May
Sowing:	Sow seeds in greenhouse in early Spring. Keep seedlings cool and moist and plant out in early Autumn in position where intended to flower. Alternatively, sow in position in Autumn. This will enable frosts to break down the tough seed covering and stimulate germination in the following Spring. Divide the crowns in Autumn.
Position:	Heavy soil with slight shade. Ground should be moist in Summer. Prefers clay or calcareous soil.
Note:	Sow seeds each year for continuous flowering.

Primrose

Coltsfoot

Tussilago farfara

Ass's Foot, Baccy Plant, Bull's Foot, Clutterclogs, Foal Foot, Son-afore-the-Father, Sweep's Brushes, Wild Rhubarb.

Edith Holden's first mention of the Coltsfoot was during a particularly mild Spring, and this is typical of the habit of the plant. It only requires one good day of sunshine in an otherwise dull wintry spell to trigger off a veritable explosion of blooms. Its curious habit of flowering before the arrival of the leaves has led to the plant's traditional name of 'Son-afore-the-Father' – a name, but not a habit, shared with the Crocus.

Used since Roman times and almost up to the present day, as a cure for coughs, Coltsfoot's scientific name comes from the Greek *tussis*, meaning a cough. Even the Indians of North America were known to have used the roots, boiled or eaten raw for the alleviation of coughs. It was considered so important, medicinally, that it was adopted as the sign for apothecaries and painted above the doorways to their shops.

Whilst the young leaves and flowers can be used in salads and soups, it is the plant's beneficial effects on bronchial and asthmatic complaints which have concerned man most. Leaves gathered in Summer, and dried, were made into herb cigarettes and tobacco for asthma sufferers, and with treacle and brown sugar into rock or lozenges for the same purpose. John Pechey, in his *Compleat Herbal*, writes that the down from the leaves was made into tinder when tinder-boxes were popular. The down was 'wrapped in a Rag, boyled a little in Lee, adding a little Salt-Petre, and dried in the Sun.'

Perennial	
Size:	3 – 12in (7.5 – 30cm)
Flowers:	March/April
Leaves:	May – July
Sowing:	Sow seeds in Autumn where intended to flower the following Spring. Alternatively, plant rhizomes from established plant in position in October or February.
Position:	In a sunny position, although later shade will not restrict them as they flower before most trees.
Note:	Restrict the growth as rhizomes spread very easily. Plant other taller, stronger growing plants nearby.

Coltsfoot

Daisy

Bellis perennis

Bairnwort, Billy Button, Eye of Day, Flower of Spring, Herb Margaret, Little Star, Miss Modesty, Open Eye, Trembling Star, Twelve Disciples.

The 'daysie' beloved of Chaucer derives its name from the Anglo Saxon *daeges-eye* meaning, quite literally, the *day's-eye* – the first flower to appear each day.

Daisy was also a common variant of the girl's name Margaret, possibly from the old French name for the plant, *marguerite*, a name which applies now to the cultivated rather than to the wild Daisy. Marguerite led in time to the English calling it 'herb Margaret', a reference to St Margaret of the Dragon who, in her prayers and supplications always kept her face toward Heaven. It was also a love diviner called the 'Measure of Love', by pulling out the petals to the chant of 'she loves me, loves me not'.

Bellis perennis flowers practically all year, and Spring was popularly supposed to have started when you could plant your foot upon nine Daisies at one step. Daisies were so abundant in Culpeper's time that he believed that nature made it so common because it was such a useful plant, and certainly it has been considered as something of a cure-all and a 'wound' herb. As Chaucer wrote in the Prologue to *Legende of Goode Women,*

> Now have I thereto this condicioun
> That of alle the flowers of the mede,
> Than love I most these flowres whyte
>   and rede
> Swiche as men callen daysies in our
>   toun.

Daisy

The fresh or dried flower heads were used in the home as an infusion for catarrh, rheumatism and kidney disorders and as early as the fifteenth century used as a herb in salads, and added to soups.

Perennial	
Size:	4 – 6in (10 – 15cm)
Flowers:	April-October
Sowing:	Sow seeds in boxes or cold frame in early Spring, or in reserve bed in June and then plant outdoors in Autumn where they are intended to flower the following year. Or, sow seed *in situ* in September. Division can take place after flowering.
Position:	Borders and edges of paths. Moist soil with a degree of shade.

Periwinkle

Vinca minor and *Vinca major*

Blue Jack, Cockle, Cut-finger, Old Woman's Eye, Pinpatch, Violet-of-the-Dead.

The Periwinkle symbolised immortality to the ancient Romans who made wreaths of the flowers for both ceremonial occasions and, perversely, for the adornment of the heads of those condemned to death. A form of mock crowning.

The Latin name for the Periwinkle, *vincula*, meaning a band, referred to the plant's long twining stems.

Whilst the Romans probably introduced the Periwinkle to Britain primarily as a medicinal plant, the custom of mocking those about to die persisted.

A garland fashioned of Periwinkles was placed upon the head of the unfortunate Simon Fraser as he was led through London on his way to his execution in 1306, and in certain parts of Britain the Periwinkle was popularly known as the 'Flower-of-the-Dead'.

Early medical manuscripts allude to the venereal qualities of the Periwinkle. According to Culpeper, Venus owned

this herb and a fourteenth century treatise recommended that the Periwinkle, when powdered with earthworms, would make an excellent food to induce love between a husband and wife.

In Elizabethan times the plant was popular for the relief of many ailments and if a garland of the flowers were hung around the neck it would prevent bleeding of the nose. But, according to Hannah Woodly in 1680, this practice was only successful if the wearer were a Christian!

Although both *Vinca minor* and *Vinca major* have been used for many years in the treatment of catarrh, dyspepsia and stomach ailments, its use is definitely not advised without medical supervision.

Perennial	
Size:	12 – 24in (30 – 60cm)
Flowers:	March – May
Sowing:	Sow under glass in Feb/ March in temperature of 65–70°. Prick off young plants into small pots, harden off in cold frame and plant out in flowering position in May for following year. Shoots root wherever they touch the ground. Cut from main plant and replant root system in new flowering position.
Position:	Moist, sandy soil in open, sunny situation in partial shade.
Note:	Makes excellent ground cover, although *Vinca major* is very invasive.

Blue and White Periwinkles

Moschatel

Adoxa moschatellina

Fairy's Clock, Good Friday Flower, Lady's Mantle, Monkweed, Musk Weed, Townhall Clock, Whiskers.

Wood Moschatel

The tiny little Moschatel, only 2 – 4 inches tall (5 – 10cm), is a rather curious plant. It is the only species of the only genus of a family all to itself; the *Flora of the British Isles* says 'of obscure relationships'. At one time it was lumped in with the Honeysuckle and Guelder Rose, but it has really no similarity to these. The Greek *adoxa* means 'obscure' or 'without glory', while the plant's specific name comes from *moschos*, 'musk', alluding to the smell of the plant when the air is damp.

Yet for all its insignificance it is a fairly common plant in Britain and on the Continent, growing in quite large numbers in woodland and mountain habitats. The majority of country names for the Moschatel have 'clock' references predominating, and the arrangement of the plant's tiny four-lobed flowers are reminiscent of the four faces of a Town Hall clock.

The plant seldom produces seeds naturally, spreading by long creeping rhizomes, so transplanting is the only means of introducing it to your garden, where it will enjoy a moist, shady position.

Daffodil

Narcissus pseudonarcissus

Bell Rose, Cuckoo Rose, Daffydowndilly, Gooseflop, Gracie Daisies, Hen and Chickens, Lent Pitchers, Queen Anne's Flowers, Yellow Maidens.

The true wild form of the Spring-flowering Daffodil has suffered greatly from years of land reclamation and the clearing of woodland but is now, fortunately, a protected plant.

The plant's generic name alludes to the famous tale of the Greek youth Narcissus, son of the river god Cephisus. The nymph Echo vied with many others of her kind for the affections of Narcissus but, regrettably, Narcissus seemed incapable of love for anyone, and being spurned Echo took her revenge by causing him to fall in love with his own reflection. He eventually died while pining away for this unattainable youth and from the ground where he lay the

Size:	9 – 10in (22.5 – 25cm)
Flowers:	March – May
Sowing:	Daffodils are best grown from bulbs. Plant in Autumn in flowering position. May take more than one year to flower but once started will be prolific; do not disturb for as long as possible. Division after flowering.
Position:	Rockeries, banks and under trees in any fibrous soil with added peat.
Note:	Do not allow air-space beneath the bulbs when planting.

Daffodil grew. Echo, in her grief for the lost Narcissus, also pined away until only her voice remained.

In Greek mythology the crown worn by Persephone, the Queen of Hell, was made of the flowers of Asphodel, but alternative spellings over many years have led, through the German *affodil* and the Dutch *de affodil*, to the present spelling. It may have been a native plant. Certainly it was known in Roman Britain yet Culpeper did not recommend it for domestic use, although it appears in homeopathic medicine where the bulb was used for respiratory diseases.

However, more use was made of the Daffodil for external ailments in the treatment of erysipelas and small cuts and abrasions. But the sap of the plant contains calcium oxalate, which can cause irritation to the skin.

Perhaps the Daffodil has been used far more often for its decorative qualities. The Belgian botanist Charles de l'Ecluse reported that so many Daffodils grew in the countryside close to London that the women of the area gathered them and then sold them in the streets of the Cheapside area, where the blooms were used to decorate all the taverns.

Daffodils

Wild Strawberry

Fragaria vesca

Wild Strawberry

It is unlikely that the origin of the name Strawberry is a development of the habit of gardeners in placing straw beneath the growing fruits, but perhaps it is more likely that it came from the older meaning of the word straw – to strew, upon the ground – or even from the straw-like appearance of the runners.

The Wild Strawberry was first mentioned in a Saxon plant list of the tenth century and records of its cultivation date from 1300. The cultivated Strawberry was not introduced into Britain until the eighteenth century.

There seem to be no particularly sinister country names for the attractive *Fragaria vesca* which is under the benign dominion of Venus and was frequently used to improve the complexion. It was used externally to combat wrinkles and freckles and a few crushed fruits, applied to the skin overnight, were thought to be instrumental in restoring beauty. Chilblains could also be prevented by rubbing the affected areas with a similar pulp during the Summer months. These remedies apart, the delicious, distinctive fruits have been used for making jams, wine and a healthy tea substitute spiced with honey and lemon, and as a general infusion to alleviate internal disorders of the stomach and kidnies.

Strawberry leaves were adopted as the symbol of English nobility, and the coronets of the grandchildren of the monarch still incorporate the Strawberry leaf. It may be that a charming country custom also bears some reference to this. Children once threaded the fruits of the Wild Strawberry on to grass stems to form circlets and bracelets.

Perennial	
Size:	2 – 12in (5 – 30cm)
Flowers:	April – June
Fruits:	June – July
Sowing:	Seeds can be sown at any time of the year. But if in an area of hard Winter weather, sow in protected area and plant out in Spring. Propagation from the runners which root into the ground at intervals. Divide from main roots and either reposition, or bring on in pots.
Position:	Good rich soil with plenty of humus. Semi-shade with moisture for the roots.

April

By all accounts Spring should now have arrived, although the weather in April can be as unpredictable as in the previous month. Wintry weather is still a definite possibility, but never likely to last very long. Yet this can often coincide with those times when most activity is planned in the garden!

April is the month when the wild flower season really gets into its stride. According to some sources the name of the month was derived from the Latin for an opening, *aperire*. In the countryside hedgerows, copses and meadows are now beginning to burgeon with many of the more familiar wild flowers, with Celandines, Violets and Periwinkles at their best and the Early Purple Orchis and Ladies Smock making a welcome appearance.

April weather and soil conditions are all important but, if these are suitable, continue planting out seedlings raised over the Winter period and sowings of later-flowering plants such as the Cranesbills and Oxeye Daisies can now take place. Good soil conditions also favour the division of certain plants and their replanting in chosen new locations.

Ground Ivy

Glechoma hederacea

Alehoof, Blue Runner, Creeping Charlie, Devil's Candlestick, Gill-go-by-the-Hedge, Hen and Chickens, Rat's Mouth, Robin-run-in-the-hedge, Tunhoof.

This dainty, perennial member of the Thyme family is not really like true ivy at all, differing both in the form of the leaves – round and heart-shaped rather than having three or five lobes – and in the profusion of violet flowers. The generic name is taken from the Greek *glechon* for mint, and simply pressing the leaves exudes a pungent, minty smell.

The leaves of Ground Ivy were formerly added to casks of beer to keep them palatable during long sea voyages.

Before the advent of hops in the late sixteenth century Ground Ivy was known as 'Alehoof' or 'Tunhoof', and was used to clarify fermenting ale. The name of Alehoof comes from the Old English name for the plant of *hofe*. It is also quite probable that the old country name for the Ground Ivy of Gill-go-by-the-Hedge actually evolved from the French word *guiller*, meaning to ferment.

It was also known in France as 'courroie de Saint-Jean', St John's Girdle, the plant being used in the making of crowns worn during the dances around the traditional bonfires on St John's Day, June 24th, therefore another of the many herbs of St John.

The minty-smelling juice extracted from the plant was frequently used to dispel migraines and headaches and a decoction of the leaves in boiling water was known as 'gill tea'. Mixed with liquorice or honey this 'tea' was used for coughs and bronchial complaints.

Perennial	
Size:	5 – 12in (12.5 – 30cm)
Flowers:	March – May
Sowing:	It is far easier to grow plants from roots or from container-grown stock. Plant roots in either Autumn or Spring. Propagation by root division at time of planting, or in Spring if existing plant developed.
Position:	Rich, moist soil in shady position which is cool.

Ground Ivy

Marsh Marigold

Caltha palustris

Bachelor's Buttons, Crazy Betsey, Gipsy's Money, Kingcup, Mary Buds, Nanny's Buttons, Publicans, Water Blebs, Yellow Boots.

In his *Herbal* of 1597 Gerard accurately described the Marsh Marigold in these terms – 'a gallant greene colour ... among which rise thicke stalkes, likewise greene, whereupon do growe goodly yellow flowers, glittering like gold'. These charming Buttercup-like flowers grow in damp woods and other similar moist habitats such as stream sides. Their commonest country name is 'King Cup', derived from the Old English 'cop' for a button – such as kings, rather than commoners, might wear. Additional references in French – 'bouton d'or', – have led to the many local names incorporating button references.

Along with the Buttercup it was believed beneficial to hang the plant above cattle byres on May Day in order to ward off evil influences and increase milk yields.

The name of Marsh Marigold actually evolved from the Old English *mersc mear gealla*, a mare, or horse blob, probably because the flowers were useful in raising blisters on horses in an early form of counter-irritation.

The charming name of 'drunkard', which came from the belief that those who picked the plant would themselves become inebriated, more probably stems from the plants close proximity to water.

While Gerard could find nothing to say regarding the medicinal properties of *Caltha palustris*, later herbalists used a tincture of Marsh Marigold leaves for the alleviation of epilepsy and anaemia. It has been used very sparingly in cooking in England, but in the United States and on the Continent the plant has been raised as a pot-herb, the leaves used as spring greens and the flower buds as capers.

Marsh Marigold

Perennial	
Size:	12 – 24in (30 – 60cm)
Flowers:	March – June
Sowing:	Sow seeds in moist compost in pots or trays in June. When large enough transfer to chosen site. Propagation by division in Autumn or Spring. But with Spring division ensure plant remains wet through the Summer. Do not allow to dry out.
Position:	Full sun. Moist, slightly acid soil. Allow at least 14in (35cm) between plants.
Note:	May also be grown in shallow water of pond site.

Lesser Celandine

Ranunculus ficaria

Brighteye, Butter and Cheese, Crazy Cup,
Frog's Foot, Gentleman's Cap and Frills,
Legwort, Starflower.

Closely resembling the Buttercup, but flowering before it, the Lesser Celandine is unrelated to the Greater Celandine, a member of the Poppy family. This similarity in common names probably caused the carver of William Wordsworth's gravestone to include upon it an image of the Greater Celandine, despite the fact that Wordsworth had written two poems to *Ranunculus ficaria*.

Both the colour of the flower and the shape of the tubers suggested various ailments and their cure. The buttery colour of the flowers and the resemblance of the tubers to cow's udders led many to believe that hanging the dried roots above cattle byres would induce greater yields of milk and butter. Yet, as Culpeper stated, 'you shall perceive the perfect image of the disease which they commonly call the piles' and although he found the plant useful in treating his daughter of scrofula – the 'King's Evil' – in a comparatively short time, the Lesser Celandine was very often used for treating piles, and gained the name 'Pilewort'.

In Elizabethan London a concoction made from the Celandine, mixed with powdered ivory, dragon water and other ingredients, was advised as a remedy against the ravages of the Plague.

If enough of the plants can be gathered they make an excellent vegetable, stewed in salt water, sautéd in butter and added to meat dishes. The leaves can also be treated as Spinach, and the buds preserved in vinegar as a substitute for capers.

Lesser Celandine

Perennial	
Size:	up to 10in (25cm)
Flowers:	March – May
Sowing:	Seeds can be sown in early March in cold frame in moist loam. When plants large enough to handle grow on outdoors and plant in September in position to flower following Spring. Divide roots in Autumn.
Position:	Shade but with Winter sun. Rich moist soil.

Wood Anemone

Anemone nemorosa

*Candlemas Caps, Cuckoo Spit, Easter
Flower, Granny-thread-the-Needle, Lady's
Nightcap, Moon-flower, Nemony, Snakes-
and-Adders, Star of Bethlehem, White
Soldiers.*

Wood Anemone
or Wind Flower

Perennial	
Size:	6 – 10in (15 – 25cm)
Flowers:	March – May
Sowing:	Sow seeds outdoors in Autumn where intended to flower. Plant roots in Autumn, in rich soil 2in (5cm) deep. Divide and transplant soon after flowering.
Position:	Ideally beneath trees to make use of leaf mould. Otherwise, rich soil with humus in shade-dappled area.
Note:	Do not allow to dry out while still in leaf.

The beautiful, almost delicate, Wood Anemone is one of the commonest of our wild flowers and one which makes a brave show towards the end of even the severest of Winters.

While some authorities claim that the ancient Greeks first named the Wood Anemone the 'Wind Flower', there is also evidence that their 'Wind Flower' was *Anemone coronaria*, the 'Garland Anemone'. However, both the generic and specific names for the Wood Anemone are from the Greek – *anemos* meaning 'wind' and *nemorosa* standing for 'of the groves' or 'woodland' – yet it is still unclear whether they might not have used *Anemone nemorosa* in the making of coronets for their festivals.

The English version was that the flower was called Wind Flower as it opened at the first command of the mild breezes of Spring, a view which Pliny shared.

According to legend Anemone was a nymph, loved by Zephyrus, who was banished by the jealous Flora and changed into a flower – one whose time of flowering should be so short that none would notice her.

The Wind Flower was an early cure for leprosy, but has been used more often for less extreme measures. According to Culpeper 'The leaves, stamped and the juices snuffed up the nose, purgeth the head mightily', and anointing the eyes with the juice of the Wood Anemone alleviated inflammation.

Ladies Smock

Cardamine pratensis

Apple Pie, Cuckoo Bread, Cuckoo Flower, Lady's Mantle, Lucy Locket, Meadow Cress, Milkmaids, Nightingale Flower, Pigeon's Eye.

Ladies Smock
or Cuckoo Flower

Ranging from white to deep lilac, the flowers of this attractive plant common to damp pastures were said to resemble female garments which had been washed and left to dry in the sun.

This was perhaps the least unsavoury of the local beliefs and country references. Yet a plant of the cuckoo season, of milkmaids – and their garments. But also a flower with a hint of more unpleasant associations.

In certain parts of France it was never used in May Day decorations as it was considered the favourite flower of adders and picking it ensured that one would be bitten by this snake before the year was out. In Germany additional ill-fortune would befall the collector as his house would surely be struck by lightning.

Cardamine came from the Greek *kardia*, the heart, and *damao*, to subdue, reference to the plant's early use in heart ailments. However, owing partly to the plant's unlucky connotations, it was rarely used in medicine until about 1700 when it figures occasionally as a help against epilepsy.

Perennial	
Size:	12 – 16in (30 – 40cm)
Flowers:	April – June
Sowing:	Sow seeds in seed compost after exposing the seed to Winter cold to break down husk. Grow seedlings on and plant out in time for Autumn or Spring flowering. Can be reproduced from the plantlets which grow upon the leaves. Lay these on soil bed in tray to develop. Plant out either in Autumn or Spring. Propagate by root division in the Autumn.
Position:	Damp soil with humus in light shade.
Note:	Ensure plant does not dry out in Summer.

Cowslip

Primula veris

Bunch-of-Keys, Cowflop, Cow Stropple, Culverkeys, Fairy Bells, Keys-of-Heaven, Palsywort, St Peter's Herb, St Peter's Keys, Tisty-tosty.

References to 'keys' and St Peter in local names point to the legend in Northern Europe that the Cowslip was the badge of St Peter. Upon hearing that a duplicate key to Heaven existed, St Peter dropped his keys, and where they fell cowslips sprang from the earth. But it appears that references to keys are far older than this legend. In Norse mythology the Cowslip was dedicated to Frega, Odin's wife, the goddess who held the keys to happiness and sexual love.

For such a pretty flower the other country names are rather inelegant. Cowslip came from the Old English *cū-slyppe* and a belief that it grew from ground covered by cow slops, and that its smell resembled a cow's breath.

It has rather been supplanted in popularity in the garden by the showier polyanthus, yet it was a great favourite with the Elizabethans for their knot gardens, and old herbals recommended the Cowslip for a variety of medicinal uses. A cure for nervous complaints, insomnia and palsy – hence 'palsywort' – it was also popular for its cosmetic qualities. Culpeper wrote that 'our city dames know well enough the ointment or distilled water of it adds to beauty ... or at least restores it when lost'. Yet these properties should be treated with care, as it was once believed that a complaint known as *primula dermatitis*, more often associated with *Primula obconica*, could result in a virulent itching if the plant came into close contact with the skin.

Cowslip

Hardy Perennial	
Size:	4 – 10in (10 – 25.5in)
Flowers:	April – May
Sowing:	Sow in rich soil in slightly warm greenhouse in Feb/March. Prick out seedlings into soil-based compost and grow on until Autumn. Transfer to flowering position for the following Spring. Divide if plot becoming overcrowded but the plant does not take kindly to moving into a less rich soil.
Position:	Prefers shade rather than full sun.

Greater Stitchwort

Stellaria holostea

*Adder's Meat, Billy White's Buttons,
Cuckoo's Meat, Jack-in-the-Lantern, Lady's
Chemise, Moonwort, One-o'clock-Popjacks,
Smocks, Star of Bethlehem, Thunderbolts.*

A conspicuous beauty of hedgerows and
banks which, owing to the plant's weak
stems, needs the protection and support
of stronger neighbouring plants.
Although it was beneficial in curing the
stitch and broken bones under the
Doctrine of Signatures, it was also
regarded as rather sinister, a plant of the
Devil and his entourage. Local names
such as Devil's Nightcap, Devil's Shirt
Buttons and Jack-in-the-Box pointed to
the suspicion with which the plant was
viewed. Anyone picking the plant would
surely be bitten by the plant's protector,
the adder, or at the very least provoke
thunder and lightning, since the Greater
Stitchwort was considered to be a
'thunder' flower, similar to the White
Campion.

Yet the Christianizing influence
ascribed the plant to the Virgin
Mary and so led to other
gentler names such as 'Star of
Bethlehem', and the plant duly
became associated with Whit Sunday.

The Greater Stitchwort protects the
pollen in the flowers in wet and thundery
weather by drooping forward.

From the gardener's point of view the
Greater Stitchwort is useful covering
against weeds but can easily be eradicated
by pulling up any new shoots.

Greater Stitchwort

Early Purple Vetch

Bitter Vetch

Lathyrus montanus

Caperoiles, Fairie's Corn, Knapperty, Napple, Nipper Nuts, Peasling, Woodpea.

The Vetches, natives of Britain and Europe, were recorded as long ago as the Anglo-Saxon era, and were in common use in Scotland since earliest times, although the first written record of the existence of the Bitter Vetch in England stems from William Turner. In 1548 he commented that in Holland the Bitter Vetch (as we know it) was called 'Erde nut'. He renamed it 'Peaserthnut'.

This mention of the 'nuts' of the Bitter Vetch refers to the seed-pods, the taste of which, eaten raw, Gerard likened to chestnuts. He also enjoyed the roots, boiled and eaten as they were, nourishing 'no lesse than Parsneps', and they were not as bad for the wind as Parsnips. Indeed it was not so much the edible qualities of the pods but of the rhizome which became popular in Scotland. In rural areas the pangs of hunger could be assuaged by chewing on the roots of the Bitter Vetch, and they were called 'cairmeal'. They were also used occasionally to add flavour to whisky.

The Bitter Vetch has been cultivated in the garden over the years mainly for the pretty coloured flowers, but be warned – the roots can be as invasive as those of the Bindweed.

In Holland another name for the pods was 'Tailed Mice' as they were 'black, round and long … with a peece of slender string hanging out behind'.

Greater Stitchwort

Perennial
Size:	6 – 24in (15 – 60cm)
Flowers:	April – June
Sowing:	Can be sown at almost any time of the year and in any soil. But as it needs the protection of other plants, adjust the sowing to ensure that when the plant flowers it is in position to take advantage of other, much stronger plants.
Position:	Damp soil in shady situations and in hedgerows.
Note:	Despite weak stems is very valuable in keeping weeds at bay.

Bitter Vetch

Perennial
Size:	6 – 16in (15 – 40cm)
Flowers:	April – June
Sowing:	Sow seeds in open ground where intended to flower, thin to about 4in (10cm) apart when large enough to handle. Divide in Spring.
Position:	Ordinary soil, kept moist in Summer.
Note:	Plant dies back in Winter to the rootstock.

Early Purple Orchis

Orchis mascula

Adam-and-Eve, Adder's Tongue, Devil-and-Angels, Fool's Stones, Fried Candlesticks, Long Purples, Naked Nannies, Underground Shepherd.

The Early Purple Orchis is easily recognised in woodlands during April by its central spike of purple flowers and dramatically lush green leaves spotted with dark brown.

The Purple Orchis was well-known for centuries as being considered full of aphrodisiac properties, because of the suggestively paired tubers. In ancient Greece the sex of future children was believed to be determined by eating the tubers of the plant. If the future father ate the larger tuber, boys would be born, and if the smaller tuber were eaten by the mother, girls. These aphrodisiac qualities were such a common belief that the tubers have been carried around the neck as love charms and Turner, writing in 1664, remarked that there were enough plants growing in Cobham Park in Kent, to 'pleasure all the seamen's wives in Rochester'. Suggestiveness apart, the plant was also known as *Gesthemane* after the belief that it grew beneath the Cross and the leaves were forever stained with the blood of Christ.

Early Purple Orchis

Perennial	
Size:	6–24in (15–60cm)
Flowers:	April/May–June
Sow:	Friends, or a nurseryman who might specialise in this plant, are the best sources for the purple orchis. *Now strictly protected by law and should never be taken from the wild.*
Position:	Situations which duplicate the natural habitat of deciduous woodland. Calcareous soil and partial shade.
Note:	Before fertilisation the purple orchis has a delightful smell somewhat like vanilla, but following pollination this smell becomes rather unpleasant.

Pasque Flower

Pulsatilla vulgaris

Blue Enomy, Coventry Bells, Dane's Blood,
Dane's Flower, Paschal Flower.

Pasque Flower

This almost exotically beautiful wild flower, a close relative of the Anemone, is yet another of the plants which is becoming rare in its natural state. In earlier centuries it was a far more common wild flower and has always been cultivated in English gardens right up to the present day. In 1551 William Turner remarked how abundant were the quantities of the Pasque flower around the Oxford area.

Originally from the French *passerfleur* – from *passer*, to excel and *fleur*, flower – the name was subsequently altered to Pasque Flower, the Flower of Easter, being the time of the year that the flower bloomed. Gerard said of it that, 'It floures for the most part about Easter, which hath moved me to name it Pasque-Floure'. The generic name *pulsatilla* refers to the 'beating' action of the flowers when disturbed by the wind, from the Latin *pulsata*.

For all its beauty it was not used by apothecaries nor mentioned in any of the Greek and Roman classic herbals.

Perhaps its main use in the past was in providing a green dye suitable for dyeing eggs at Easter time. It was mentioned, along with various other plants, for the decoration and gilding of some 400 eggs at an Easter court festival held in the reign of Edward I. It was also known by the name of 'Dane's Blood' or 'Dane's Flower' as it was supposed to rise from the blood shed in battle by Danish invaders. As many of these battles took place in terrain which well suited the Pasque Flower it is easy to make this association. The Pasque Flower grows also in America where it is called the Prairie Crocus and Prairie Smoke.

Perennial	
Size:	4 – 12in (10 – 30cm)
Flowers:	April/May
Sowing:	Sow seeds outdoors in final flowering position, as soon as ripe. Or sow seeds in boxes of seed compost in cold frame in July. When large enough transfer to pots and grow on through Winter. Plant out in the Spring, or in September for following year. Division is not recommended.
Position:	Lime or chalk. Sun and well-drained.
Note:	When planting make sure crown is not covered by soil.

Wood Crowfoot

Ranunculus auricomus

Goldilocks, Gold Cup, Gold Knobs, King's Cup, Leopard's Foot.

A member of the *Ranunculus* genus and a close relation of the Buttercup, and called Crowfoot from the resemblance of the leaves to the feet of the crow.

Crowfoot was an early name for the Buttercup before the title 'Buttercup' became common in the eighteenth century.

The Wood Crowfoot was noted for its caustic properties and more than one source relates how 'the ancients' used the sap of the Crowfoot to smear the points of their arrows to make them poisonous. However, the root of another double version of the Crowfoot, known as St Anthony, was also considered to be a cure for the plague and lunacy. Culpeper did not consider the Crowfoot beneficial except to raise blisters, and beggars in the Middle Ages are thought to have smeared their sores with the sap to elicit more sympathy. But the Crowfoot is still dangerous to cattle, and to man in some degree.

Perhaps Pliny was the only one to speak, slightly guardedly, of its qualities. He observed that anyone eating the plant would be overcome by laughter to such an extent that if he did not then drink pine kernels and pepper in date wine he well might 'guffaw his way into the next world in a most unseemly manner'.

Despite this, the Crowfoot, in one form or another, has graced gardens for centuries so that there are now many varieties available under the Crowfoot name.

Wood Crowfoot

Common Avens

Common Avens

Geum urbanum

Blessed Herb, Colewort, Gold Star, Ram's Foot, Star of the East, Yellow Strawberry.

The Common Avens was also known as Herb Bennet, from the medieval Latin *herba benedicta* a herb ascribed to St Benedict, the founder of the Benedictine Order of monks. St Benedict was once handed a cup of poisoned wine by a fellow monk and, upon blessing it, the cup broke into pieces.

Certainly the sweet, spicy smell of the roots were said to repel evil and, in the *Ortis Sanitatis* published in Mainz in 1491, we read that, 'if the root is in the home, the Devil is powerless and flees from it'.

The flower's five golden petals also suggested the traditional five wounds of Christ and this, together with other religious associations, led to the Common Avens appearing so frequently in church carvings.

Culpeper recommended the plant as a wholesome and healthful herb and, apart from the frequent use of the plant as a moth repellant – the roots dug up in autumn, thoroughly dried and used as required – the Common Avens has been used for several medicinal purposes.

It was the 'Kind Herb' much sought after by all animals as it helped the stomach, liver and heart. In the seventeenth century a decoction in wine, or pottage, was used against upset stomach, wind, stitch and the bites of 'venomous beasts'. Modern herbalists agree that it is useful for its astringent qualities as a mouthwash for gingivitis.

The fruits of *Geum urbanum* are hooked, a possible reason for the actual name of 'Avens', from the Anglo Saxon *awelan*, a diminutive of *awel*, a hook.

Wood Crowfoot

Perennial
Size:	Up to 12in (30cm)
Flowers:	April – June
Sowing:	Sow seeds in open ground in either Autumn or Spring where intended to flower. Plants can be set out in flowering positions any time during the Winter. Division not necessary until the clump becomes overcrowded.
Position:	Requires a moist soil. Ordinary loam and protection from the cold winds.

Common Avens

Perennial
Size:	12 – 24in (30 – 60cm)
Flowers:	June – August.
Sow:	Sow in cold frame in March. When seedlings large enough prick out and transfer to nursery bed. Plant out in Autumn or over-winter in cold frame for Spring planting. Divide in Spring or at planting time.
Position:	Herbaceous border in any good garden soil, slightly moist. Prefer shade from neighbouring plants.
Note:	Can fail if in heavy soil during hard Winter.

Wild Arum

Arum maculatum

Adam-and-Eve, Adder's Tongue, Babe-in-the-Cradle, Calve's Foot, Cuckoo-pint, Dog's Dibble, Jack-in-the-Pulpit, Moll of the Woods, Parson and Clerk, Priest's Hood, Sweethearts, Wake Robin.

Surely, in appearance, the most curious of the British wild flowers. Within a fleshy green-white sheath, a central spadix arises with the male and female flowers hidden around the base. This spadix emits a slight smell of carrion and the plant is pollinated by carrion flies. Apart from the belief that the height of the spadix revealed the success of the coming year's crops, the Wild Arum has always had sexual connotations, many reflected in country names and due mainly to the form of the spadix. According to some authorities the term 'Cuckoo-pint' should more aptly be 'Cuckold', rather than any reference to the cuckoo.

A series of tapestries made for the marriage of Francis I of France in 1514, relating the hunt and capture of a unicorn, contain background detail composed entirely of plants with sexual inferences.

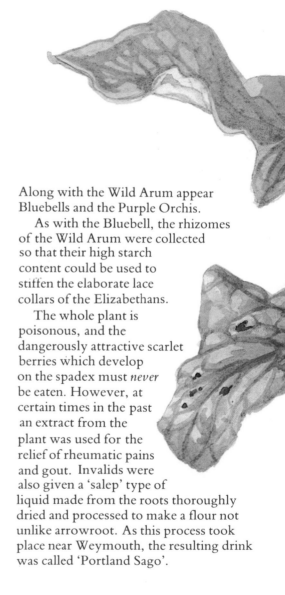

Along with the Wild Arum appear Bluebells and the Purple Orchis.

As with the Bluebell, the rhizomes of the Wild Arum were collected so that their high starch content could be used to stiffen the elaborate lace collars of the Elizabethans.

The whole plant is poisonous, and the dangerously attractive scarlet berries which develop on the spadex must *never* be eaten. However, at certain times in the past an extract from the plant was used for the relief of rheumatic pains and gout. Invalids were also given a 'salep' type of liquid made from the roots thoroughly dried and processed to make a flour not unlike arrowroot. As this process took place near Weymouth, the resulting drink was called 'Portland Sago'.

Perennial	
Size:	12 – 18in (30 – 45cm)
Flowers:	April/May
Sowing:	Plant tubers in any good garden soil, about 6in (15cm) deep in Autumn. Divide clumps in August/September.
Position:	Part shade from shrubs and trees. Moist, well-drained.

Wild Arum,
Cuckoo Pint or
Lords and Ladies

Red and White Dead-nettles

Lamium purpureum and *Lamium album*

Red Dead-nettle: *Archangel, Bad Man's Posies, Bumble-bee Flower, Rabbit's Meat, Stinking Weed.*
White Dead-nettle: *Deaf Nettle, Adam-and-Eve-in-a-Bower, Helmet Flower, Snake's Flower.*

Whilst the Dead-nettles do not have the same reputation as the Stinging Nettle for medical or culinary purposes, they were used for a number of ailments. The effects were astringent and diuretic, with the White Dead-nettle being particularly sought after for female disorders, diarrhoea and catarrh. Today it is used in homeopathy for kidney complaints.

Although the Dead-nettles can be eaten in similar ways to the Stinging Nettle perhaps the most charming manner was the ancient habit which appealed to children. They picked the white flowers and sucked them to extract the honey within. This led to the country name of 'Suck Bottle'. One other country name, which becomes clear when the flowers of White Dead-nettle are looked at closely, was 'Adam-and-Eve-in-a-Bower'. Two black stamens hang down from the topmost hooded lip which, if the flower is then turned upside down, give an appearance of two people in a 'bed'.

White Dead-nettle

Red Dead-nettle

Red Dead-nettle	
Annual	
Size:	4 – 18in (10 – 45cm)
Flowers:	March – October
White Dead-nettle	
Perennial	
Size:	8 – 24in (20 – 60cm)
Flowers:	May – December
Sowing:	Seeds can be sown in Spring in open ground where intended to flower. Plant in either Autumn or Spring. Propagation of *Lamium album* by division at time of planting.
Position:	Ordinary garden soil which does not dry out completely in either sun or partial shade.

May

Often referred to as the 'gateway to Summer' the month of May possesses all the joy of Spring together with the firm promise of the Summer to come.

May Day has been celebrated since Roman times, and from Medieval and Tudor days the practices of 'bringing in the may' and decorating the 'may pole' have been traditional customs. May Day was also the occasion for placing sprays of wild flowers above cattle sheds and farm dwellings to ensure both protection from evil influences and to increase yields.

Bluebells, Ransoms and the gentle Wood Sorrel now carpet woodlands and are very often found in the same situations as the prolific Red Campion Although the Meadow Buttercup is more often associated with June other members of the genus, Wood Crowfoot and the Spearwort, are now evident.

With the more predictable weather many wild flower seeds can now be sown direct into their flowering positions in open ground. But even though some days may still be rather inclement there is also a danger that with the increasing strength of the sun certain plants may dry out under long periods of sunshine, so be prepared to water well during this time.

Bluebell

Hyacinthoides non-scripta

Bell Bottles, Blue Bonnets, Cuckoo's Boots, Crowbells, Goosie-Gander, Jacinth, Rook's Flowers.

It is now illegal to dig up the roots of the Bluebell. Although prolific amounts still carpet woodlands and hillsides in Spring they are yet another species of wild flower in danger of over-picking. Yet the greater danger to this familiar and beautiful flower comes more from the trampling down of the leaves than from the actual gathering of the flowers. If the leaves are destroyed, then the plant will receive no food.

There has always been certain confusion regarding the Latin name of the Bluebell, as much as there is about the actual source of its name. The Bluebell or Wild Hyacinth, *Hyacinthoides non-scripta*, has been known by various generic names: *Scilla non-scriptus* from the nodding quality of the flowers and *Endymion non-scriptus* after the Greek youth loved by Silene, the goddess of the Moon.

However, the legend of Endymion is only one of several such legends regarding the Bluebell.

Pliny wrote that the flower sprang from the blood of Ajax, the hero of the Trojan War who killed himself after Achilles' armour was given to Odysseus. Yet a more prevalent tale ascribes the plant to Hyacinthus. He was loved by both Apollo and Zephyrus, the god of the west wind. This proved unfortunate for the youth, as he loved Apollo the more and Zephyrus, in a jealous rage, slew the youth. Once again, as with the other

legends, the Bluebell sprang forth from the very ground where the blood was spilt.

The leaves of this plant were further thought to bear small markings which were interpreted as the Greek words 'ai ai' meaning alas.

But although the marked variety still grows in parts of Greece the Bluebells of Northern Europe are of the unmarked or 'non-scriptus' variety.

A variety of names and a variety of legends. Perhaps Tennyson summed it up best,

What is it? A learned man,
    Could give it a clumsy name,
Let him name it who can,
    The beauty would be the same.

William Turner first mentions the use of the bulbs for glue and, as with the Wild Arum, the starch obtained was used to stiffen the elaborate collars of the Elizabethans.

Whereas the Bluebell is a common plant in England, it is unrelated to the Bluebell of Scotland, this title referring to the Harebell. In the United States both the Virginia Cowslip and the Bellflower are also referred to as Bluebells.

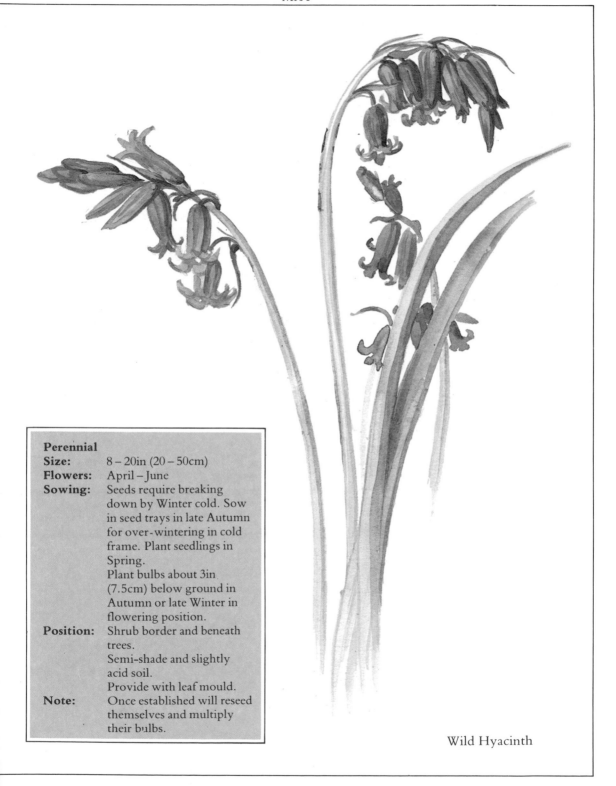

Perennial
Size: 8 – 20in (20 – 50cm)
Flowers: April – June
Sowing: Seeds require breaking
down by Winter cold. Sow
in seed trays in late Autumn
for over-wintering in cold
frame. Plant seedlings in
Spring.
Plant bulbs about 3in
(7.5cm) below ground in
Autumn or late Winter in
flowering position.
Position: Shrub border and beneath
trees.
Semi-shade and slightly
acid soil.
Provide with leaf mould.
Note: Once established will reseed
themselves and multiply
their bulbs.

Wild Hyacinth

Red Campion

Silene dioica

*Adder's Flower, Bull Rattle, Devil's Flower,
Red Gramfer-Greggles, Jack-by-the-Hedge,
Red Mintchop, Plum Pudding, Scalded
Apples, Lousy Soldiers Buttons, Water
Poppies.*

In Springtime the Red Campion will
often share not only the same habitat as
the Hyacinth and the Early Purple Orchis
but also certain similar country names.

Campion might well be a rather
obscure version of 'Champion', even

though the leaves used to make crowns
for successful athletes were more likely to
have come from the genus *Lychnis* –
Ragged Robin and Catchfly.

The present generic name *Silene* refers
the plant to the Greek god Silenus, the
foremost satyr, often shown riding upon
a donkey in an inebriated state. Yet the
Red Campion is a plant with a darker
side. It was one of the Devil's plants and
caused untimely death if picked. One
local tradition had it that if the Red
Campion were picked, then death waited
upon the father, and if the White
Campion were the picked flower, death
chose the mother.

While being similar in appearance, save
for the colour of the flowers, the Red and
White Campions differ in other ways.
Whereas the Red Campion opens in the
daytime and is scentless, the White
Campion only opens at dusk and has a
very pronounced scent. Again, the Red
Campion has flowers of only one sex,
hence the scientific name *dioica* – having
male and female organs on separate plants
There is also the possibility that where
both grow together a hybrid pink or pale
red Campion may result.

Red Campion

Perennial
Size:	12 – 36in (30 – 90cm)
Flowers:	May – August
Sowing:	Sow seeds under glass or in greenhouse February/ March in medium temperature, prick out young plants and grow on in cooler temperature. Alternatively, sow direct in flowering position in April. Sowing in Autumn may be unsuccessful if the Winter is severe.
Position:	Ordinary garden soil, partial shade. Border plant.

Wild Parsley

Hardy Biennial
Size:	8 – 15in (20 – 45cm)
Flowers:	June – August
Sowing:	Sow seeds in seedbed in March and in succession throughout Summer. Thin to 3in (8cm).
Position:	Full sun and even semi-shade. Will grow well if backed by wall or rocks. Rich, fine and moist soil.
Note:	Will be hard to grow in heavy soil, as seedlings are weak.

Wild Parsley

Petroselinum crispum

Although the Parsley was very familiar to the ancient Greeks and Romans there is no definite record of Parsley growing in England before Elizabethan times. It has been suggested that it was introduced during the Middle Ages, but there are indications that the Anglo-Saxons used it in a concoction for a 'broken head'. Whereas many of today's vegetables and plants are considered improvements of the earlier wild species, in the case of Parsley the wild flower is an escapee from areas where the cultivated Parsley had previously existed.

Parsley has been associated with many tales over the years. In one early belief you could pronounce a sentence of death on your enemy if you declared his name while pulling a root of Parsley out of the ground, and the saying that someone was 'in need of parsley' meant that they were so ill that they were likely to die. Associations with death may well have come from the idea that the plant stemmed from the blood of Archemorus, the 'Forerunner of Death'. *Petroselinum* comes from the Greek meaning 'rock celery' but over the years has developed through medieval English *persele* to the later *perseley*.

A famous culinary herb, Parsley is rich in iron, calcium, vitamins and other trace elements and apart from being a valuable addition to dishes has also been used as an infusion to relieve cramps and aid the digestion.

However, growing Parsley can be difficult. But if, according to the legends you take it 'seven or nine times to the Devil' and if the seeds are sown on Good Friday, and if it is only planted by a good and honest man, then you may be successful. It might be wise to bear in mind, however, that:

> When the mistress is the master
> The Parsley will grow faster.

Wild Beaked Parsley

Red Campion

Lesser Spearwort

Ranunculus flammula

Butterplate, Cowgrass, Goose Tongues,
Water Buttercup, Snake's Tongues,
Yellow Crane.

There are two Spearworts, the Lesser and the Greater. The Greater Spearwort is the largest member of the Buttercup family with large impressive flower heads, anything up to one and a half inches in diameter.

Both of the Spearworts prefer damper situations than the rest of the Buttercups and are often found beside ditches, streams and in boggy areas.

The specific name for the Lesser Spearwort is *flammula*, meaning a little flame, and refers to the acridity of the sap from the plant. This property was put to good use by beggars in the Middle Ages. They would smear the sap on cuts and sores in order to inflame them and so elicit more sympathy from ordinary people. Neither of the Spearworts were of any great medicinal significance except, perhaps, that some doctors have claimed

Lesser Spearwort

Perennial	
Size:	6 – 18in (15 – 45cm)
Flowers:	May – September
Sowing:	Sow seeds in Spring in open ground where intended to flower. Planting of seedlings can take place either in Spring or Autumn. Division in the Spring.
Position:	Damp soil, slightly acid. Sun or partial shade.
Note:	Greater Spearwort may be grown in the same manner.

that the sap from the plant is extremely effective in causing vomiting in anyone poisoned, the theory being that the lesser poison would drive out the greater.

Germander Speedwell

Veronica chamaedrys

Angel's Eye, Blue Stars, Eye-of-Christ, Jerrymander, Lamb's Lettuce, Llewelyn's Flower, Mother-breaks-her-Heart, Remember Me, Pick-your-Mother's-eye-out, Wish-me-Well.

Germander Speedwell

The legend of St Veronica – who wiped Christ's brow on his passage to the Cross with her handkerchief and found the image of the Saviour's face had become fixed on the cloth – is reputed to have given the generic name *veronica* to the Speedwell family of plants. There is also a story that Llewelyn adopted it as his flower to lend success to his ventures. But either the plant's ability to cure ailments quickly, or the fact that the petals soon fall away after picking, are more likely to have prompted folk to call the plant Speedwell, in the sense of 'farewell' or 'goodbye'.

Geoffrey Grigson in *An Englishman's Flora* relates an old, yet rather savage, country custom which was once well-known in both England and Germany. One child would induce another to pick a Germander Speedwell. When the petals fell away soon after picking that unfortunate child would be informed that he had caused his mother's heart to break by plucking the flower.

In fact, dire consequences followed any picking of the flower. It could lead to the birds descending and plucking out your eyes, the country name of 'Bird's Eye' alludes to this, a stranger would take revenge upon you, and at the very least, your actions would cause a storm to develop. Yet, conversely, in Ireland the wearing of Speedwell was believed to keep the wearer free from any accident.

Several of the Speedwells were once used as substitutes for tea. This was a more common practice on the Continent than in England where it was recommended as a cure for those inbibing too much ale and those of 'a gross habit of body'. Yet the Speedwell was noted more for its property of relieving sore eyes and its ability to sharpen the vision.

Perennial	
Size:	3 – 16in (7 – 40cm)
Flowers:	May – June
Sowing:	Either in Autumn or Early Spring where intended to flower. Thin to 6in (15cm) apart. Divide in Spring so that clumps do not become overcrowded.
Position:	Hedge banks in almost any soil with partial shade.

Ramsons

Allium ursinum

Badger's Flower, Brandy Bottles, Gipsy's Gibbles, Iron Flower, Ramsden, Ram's Horn, Stink Plant, Wild Leek.

The leaves of *Allium ursinum*, Wild Garlic or Ramsons, resemble those of many other members of the Lily family, in particular the Lily-of-the-Valley. The plants carpet the floors of shady woodland in late Spring and early Summer giving off a distinctive odour, especially when crushed, which led to them being called 'Ramsons', after the Old Norse *ramse* and the English *hramsa* – likening the odour to that of the unpleasant smelling ram. 'Ramsons', in turn, led to the naming of certain towns in England where the Wild Garlic grew in significant quantities.

All the various Garlics were reputed to have great curative properties. As John Aubrey put it,

'Eat Leekes in March and Ramsons in
    May
And all the year Physicians may play'

The specific name *ursinum* came from the Latin for a bear, which may have been a way of signifying its inferiority – in the same way that 'dog' was applied to certain plants – or from the popular belief that not only were the leaves similar in appearance to the ears of a bear, but that bears had a fondness for the plant.

Perennial	
Size:	3 – 18in (7.5 – 45cm)
Flowers:	April – June
Sowing:	Growing from seed may take 3 years for flower to develop. Bulbs should be planted in Autumn or Spring in flowering position, in groups, 2in (5cm) deep. Do not disturb, but divide soon after flowering.
Position:	Away from the house and preferably down wind. Rich moist soil but well-drained, in sunny position.
Note:	A spreading plant so confine to 'wild' areas.

Wild Garlic

Common Broom

Broom

Cytisus scoparius

*Banadle, Bannel, Green Basom, Brushes,
Cat's Peas, Golden Chair, Lady's Slipper,
Witch's Flower.*

Hard, stiff and unbending but synonymous with witches, and also a symbol of royalty. The use of the broom plant bound around a stave, or piece of wood, and used to sweep floors, has naturally led to us adopting the name for a common domestic item.

It was believed that the Broom plant also furnished witches with their means of transportation through the skies and yet Broom was also powerful in combating these same witches.

Broom was adopted as the symbol of Henry II who had doubtless heard that his grandfather, Fulke of Anjou, wore a spray of Broom on his way to the Holy Land during the Crusades, a symbol handed down to his son Geoffrey, and Broom was the ancient *planta genista* from which the Plantagenets took their name.

Broom was considered beneficial to sheep. John Aubrey states that farmers grew it close to grazing land because if the sheep ingested the flowers and shoots, it would 'keep them sound', and shepherds in the Auvergne also believed that their sheep gained protection from adder bites by so doing. It is not surprising that modern science has now confirmed that an alkaloid of Broom does, in fact, render snake bites harmless.

The young tips of the branches and the flowers have been made into both a soothing tea and wine. The ashes of Broom could also be infused in wine as a cure for dropsy.

Perennial/Deciduous shrub
Size: 36 – 64in (90 – 180cm)
Flowers: May – June
Sowing: Seeds may be sown in open ground in Spring or into pots, and planted out when large enough to handle. Plant young shrubs in Spring just prior to new growth starting. Prune by cutting back new growth in July after flowering.
Position: Lime free soil. Warm, dry soil particularly sand and gravel. Hedging plant.

Wood Sorrel

Oxalis acetosella

Alleluia, Cheese and Bread, Cuckoo Meat, Green Sauce, Green Snob, Lady's Clover, Sleeping Beauty, Sour Sally, Whitsun Flower.

Wood Sorrel

A plant closely associated with the cuckoo as the bird was believed to eat the leaves, in order to clear its throat for singing in the Spring.

Even though William Turner has been given the credit for naming the plant 'Alleluia' because, as he put it 'It appeareth about Easter, when Alleluia is sung again', it is also possible that the name he used came from 'Juliola', a name common in Southern Italy. The Wood Sorrel is a rather curious plant. It has two distinct sets of flowers. The spring flowers are occasionally visited by bees, but the later summer flowers never open. The spring flowers also close up during rainfall and at night, which led to one of the local names of 'Sleeping Beauty'.

The Wood Sorrel's generic name was derived from *oxys*, the Greek for 'bitter' and *hals*, 'salt', and the plant has a high oxalic acid content which renders the taste rather bitter and should be used sparingly.

It also received the country name of 'Green Sauce' and Deering related how country folk 'Beat the herb to a mash and mixed with Vinegar and Sugar, eat it as Sauce for roasted meat'. Small amounts of the leaves can be used in salads or soup, but enjoyment might be tempered slightly by the knowledge that the North American Indians once fed the Wood Sorrel to their horses to give them greater speed.

Perennial	
Size:	4–6in (10–15cm)
Flowers:	May–July
Sowing:	Sow seeds in early Spring where they are to flower, thinning later in the year to about 6in (15cm). Take offsets in Spring, replanting in chosen position.
Position:	Acid soil. Moist, with partial shade.

Alkanet

Pentaglottis sempervirens

Bird's Eye, Pheasant's Eye, Blue-eyed Mary.

A member of the Forget-me-Not family and rather reminiscent of Borage, although the flowers of Borage have conspicuous black stamens at the centre while the flowers of Green Alkanet are round-edged and funnel shaped with no central black stamen.

Alkanet comes from the French *orchanette* and from the Arabic *al-henna*. Alkanet was the plant that supplied the red dye henna which was a great favourite with Egyptian women for colouring their hair and nails. Throughout the years Alkanet has been confused with Borage, and the Alkanet which Edith illustrated was believed to be an introduced species from medieval times. It is probable that monks introduced Alkanet into Britain for the red dye it produced and which was later used to colour inferior wines.

It was called *Anchusa sempervirens* by the botanist Linnaeus but this was reclassified to *Pentaglottis* by Tausch. A plant with no specific medical properties, Gerard referred to it as the 'everliving Borage'. Following planting of Alkanet in the Tradescant Garden in Lambeth in 1656 it was later recorded as one of the few original plants still growing there a hundred years later.

As with Borage the green shoots of Alkanet can be cooked and eaten rather like spinach, and a drug obtained from it has, on occasions, been tried for the treatment of nervous disorders.

Evergreen Alkanet

Perennial	
Size:	12 – 40in (30 – 100cm)
Flowers:	May – June
Sowing:	Sow the seeds middle to late Summer under glass. The young plants should be wintered over and planted out in the Spring. Allow about 12in (30cm) space. Or plant outdoors in Autumn, but protect in Winter. Propagate by root cuttings or division in early Spring.
Position:	Ordinary soil, even in limy soil. Sunny position and well drained. If soil very wet in Winter the roots will rot.

Heartsease

Viola tricolor

Call-me-to-you, Herb Trinity, Kiss-me-behind-the-garden-hedge, Kiss-me-Kitty-run-the-street, Love-in-idleness, Tittle-my-Fancy, Pinkeney John, Three-faces-under-one-hood.

The delightful little Heartsease rejoices in quite a number of charming country names, almost all of which have romantic associations. The Heartsease, or Wild Pansy, was the forerunner of the well-known cultivated Pansy. Although the Elizabethans applied the name Heartsease to *Viola tricolor*, the modern Pansy comes about from a combination of both *V. tricolor* and *V. lutea*, the Mountain Pansy, which took place during the nineteenth century.

Pansy was from the French *pensée*, and the flower was the symbol of remembrance, yet this quality applied more particularly to lovers in the case of the Heartsease.

Ophelia, in Shakespeare's *Hamlet*, said that 'there is pansies – that's for thoughts', whilst in *A Midsummer Night's Dream* Oberon anointed the eyes of the sleeping Titania with juice from the Heartsease, or 'Love-in-idleness', so that when she awoke she would instantly fall in love with Bottom.

Any plant which had so many 'love' connotations was bound to receive Christianizing names, and the three petals with their varied colours supplied the answer. The plant became known also as 'Herb Trinity'. It is interesting to note that despite the beneficial effects which the plant had on the heart, in more ways than one, Culpeper mentions it as being particularly effective and 'an excellent cure for venereal disease'.

Common
Bugle

Yellow Heartsease

Bugle
Ajuga reptans

Baby's Rattle, Carpenter's Herb, Herbflower, Horse and Hound, Nelson's Bugle, Self-heal, Thunder-and-Lightning, Wild Mint.

An attractive, common wild flower which grows well on slightly moist ground and, in its natural habitat, beneath trees. Clusters of bluish, mauve flowers stand up to a foot high on a central, slightly hairy stem.

The common name of Bugle refers less to the actual shape of the flowers and their resemblance to the musical instrument, or even a passing similarity to the glass decoration sometimes sewn into clothes, than to an adulteration of the various names over many years. The origin is obscure, but through the Latin *bugula*, to *ajuga*, the final common name of Bugle probably evolved.

Gerard mentions that the Bugle was cultivated in gardens in Elizabethan times but it has certainly fallen from popularity over the years. Several country names point to *Ajuga reptans* being used primarily as a 'wound' herb for cuts, bruises and the like. Both Pechey and Culpeper sang the plant's praises as a healer of external and, occasionally, internal wounds. An interesting sidelight is that it was believed to counter the disasterous effects of *dementia tremens*.

In the garden it is best to treat it with care. Like the Mint, it can get out of hand and spread by its creeping runners, the shoots from the plant rooting and then budding at the point where the leaf is attached to the stem.

Heartsease	
Perennial	
Size:	3 – 4in. (7.5 – 10cm)
Flowers:	April – August
Sowing:	Seeds sown direct into open ground in Spring are not as satisfactory as sowing in late Summer in cold frame to over-winter in protected area. Plant out in chosen site in March. Alternatively, if plants strong enough, plant in flowering position in September/October.
Position:	Borders, although several need to be planted in a group to give a show. Partial shade or full sun. Moist, rich soil.
Note:	Heartsease are self-seeding and give a very long flowering season.

Bugle	
Perennial	
Size:	4 – 12in (10 – 30cm)
Flowers:	May – July
Sowing:	Either in Spring in flowering position or in Autumn, if protected from Winter frosts. Thin out to 4in (10cm) apart. Plant in Spring or Autumn in flowering position. Divide any time, in dry conditions.
Position:	Border plant. Ordinary soil which remains moist. Partial shade.
Note:	Plant spreads by creeping runners and needs to be restricted by stones or more dominant plants, such as the Dandelion.

Saxifrage

Saxifraga granulata

Cuckoo Flower, Fair-Maids-of-France,
Fruit of May, Rock Breaker, Sassifrax,
Snow-on-the-Mountains.

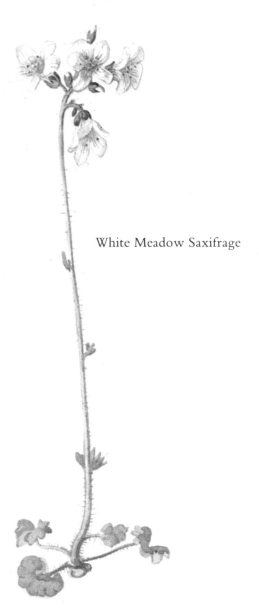

White Meadow Saxifrage

The Saxifrage family took their name from the locations in which they were found and the supposed medicinal qualities that they possessed.

Saxifrage is from the Latin *saxum* meaning a 'rock', and *frangere* to 'break'. Many kinds were found nestling in the crevices of rocks and were assumed to have shattered or broken the rock as they developed. Also the small brown, pea-like, bulbils on the plant's stem were the perfect illustration, according to the Doctrine of Signatures, of the 'stones' contained in the body. Consequently, extracts of the root were used for the treatment of gall stones and kidney stones.

However, there was once a rather more sinister aspect of the plant's supposed 'stone-breaking' quality. In Russia, in the nineteenth century, the Saxifrage was believed to release dead spirits from their graves.

The delicately flowered Saxifrage is fast disappearing from the countryside, in particular from those natural meadows which modern farming practices seek to eradicate.

The Saxifrage multiplies naturally by means of the stem bulbils and self-seeding.

Perennial	
Size:	6 – 20in (15 – 50cm)
Flowers:	April – June
Sowing:	For Spring flowering, sow seeds in Autumn in trays and over-winter in a cold frame. Or sow in open ground in Spring, but these will be less successful.
Position:	Rock gardens. Non-acid, well-drained soil. Sun or shade.

Herb Robert

Geranium robertianum

*Bloodwort, Bloody Mary, Death-come-
Quickly, Fellonwort, Granny-thread-the-
Needle, Hop-o'my-Thumb, Poor Robert,
Robin's Flower, Robin Hood, Stinking
Robert, Wren's Flower.*

According to the medieval Doctrine of
Signatures, Herb Robert was used for the
treatment of disorders of the blood,
because its stems and lower leaves turned
red in the Autumn.

Although there is a certain difference of
opinion regarding the origin of its name,
it was probably dedicated to the eleventh
century French ecclesiastic St Robert, the
founder of the Cistercian order of monks.

Herb Robert is a member of the
Cranesbill family but differs from the
others in having rounded petals and
ragged leaves. One country name for the
plant is Ragged Robin, yet it should not
be confused with *Lychnis flos-cuculi*.

References to Robin in local names
point to the plants association with the
sinister John Hood and Robin Hood. In
fact, the greater majority of local names
bear uncomfortable associations. Add the
bloody effect of the leaves and the
'loathsome, stinking smell' as Culpeper
called it, and it does not appear a very
attractive plant.

Such was not the case in either
Wordsworth's estimation, nor yet that of
the early herbalists, who found it useful
since earliest times for external bruises
and grazing. Crushed, it acts as a
powerful mosquito repellant and the juice
of the leaves can be infused, steeped and
used to eradicate head lice.

Herb Robert

Annual or Biennial

Size:	4 – 18 in (10 – 45cm)
Flowers:	May – September
Sowing:	Sow in flowering position in March, or in reserve bed in Summer and then plant out in the Autumn in position chosen for flowering next Spring. Division in Spring or Autumn.
Position:	Any garden soil, preferably damp. Semi-shade, hedgerows and walls.

Treacle Mustard

Erysimum cheiranthoides

Wormseed.

Treacle Mustard is also known as Wormseed and is another of the wild flowers which frequent waste ground.

The common name comes down from the Greek word "*theriaki*", which stood for an antidote to poison and particularly the bites from poisonous insects and animals. The specific name is shared with the Wallflower genus of plants, *Cheiranthoides* coming from *cheiranthus*

meaning a 'hand–flower' and a reference to the fact that they were the flowers carried in bouquets and posies at festivals and ceremonies. The modern *Cheiranthus* plants are the familiar garden Wallflowers.

It is not a very dramatic or even beautiful plant, yet was very popular for its medicinal qualities in the Middle Ages. Then it was combined with 72 other herbs and the whole made up into the famous poison-antidote 'Venice Treacle'. The plant achieved the 'wormseed' name from the supposed ability to drive out 'worms' in young children. But perhaps Culpeper summed up the plant best: 'It is an annual about two feet high with long slender roots, long narrow leaves and small yellow flowers produced in a spike. The seed is born in vessels resembling pea pods. Used nowadays in small amounts as a laxative. Made into a syrup with honey and a little vinegar beneficial to asthma. Small doses of the juice given in white wine promotes the menses and hasten the delivery of the child!'

Treacle Mustard or
Jack-by-the-Hedge

Annual or Biennial	
Size:	8 – 36in (20 – 90cm)
Flowers:	June – August
Sowing:	Sow seeds in Spring or Autumn where intended to flower, thin to 6in (15cm). Or sow seeds in cold frame in September and the following Spring transfer plants to flowering position.
Position:	Full sun or partial shade. Good garden soil.

June

Essentially *the* mid-Summer month and frequently containing some of the hottest and driest days of the year. This is the time when all nature, and wild flowers in particular, are at their most luxuriant, presenting a rich variety of blooms in meadows, woodland and hedgerows. The flowers of the Wild Rose festoon hedge banks, Foxgloves are now evident in increasing numbers, and the evening air is scented with Honeysuckle, Red and White Clover and Ladies Bedstraw. Also a very active time for butterflies and moths.

Many June flowers will already have been started either under glass earlier in the year or in their flowering positions in early Spring, but with the chance of long, sunny days with occasional very hot weather it is essential to ensure that plants do not dry out but are provided with plenty of moisture, and weeds should be kept in check.

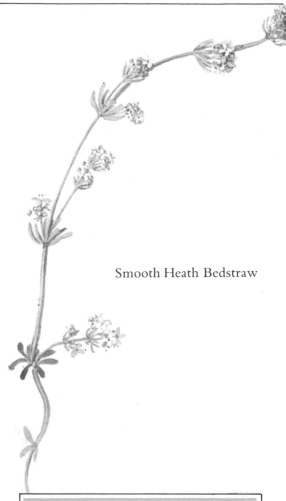

Smooth Heath Bedstraw

Ladies Bedstraw

Galium verum

Creeping Jenny, Fleaweed, Golden Dust, Gallion, Maiden's Hair, Strawbed, Petty Mugget, Cheese Rennet, Wild Rosemary.

Ladies Bedstraw is a tall, rather straggling plant with a mass of small, bright yellow flowers which, with its narrow needle-like dark green leaves, distinguishes it from other members of the Bedstraw family.

The flowers smell like honey after dusk and of hay when the plant is cut down and dried. Because of the pleasant smell it was used to stuff bedding in earlier times. It was also easy to burn once used, fleas did not like it and it was in plentiful supply. According to legend Bedstraw formed the bed upon which the Virgin Mary lay at the Nativity and this led to the belief that beds of *Galium verum* were beneficial during childbirth. In some European countries further protection was given to nursing mothers if they carried a spray inside their shoes. Something of the same practice extended also to weary travellers. Road-weary feet could be revived by immersing them in a bowl of Ladies Bedstraw infused in boiling water. Although used rarely today the plants main medical attribute was in the prevention of internal bleeding and nose bleeds. *Galium verum* actually contains a chemical which can be made into the drug *dicouramil* – also found in Sweet Woodruff – which prevents the blood from clotting.

Of no great culinary importance, Bedstraw was used for curdling the milk in cheese making, giving it the name of 'Cheese Rennet'. It will pay to encourage this plant in the garden as it is the main food plant of the Elephant Hawk Moth.

Perennial
Size:	6 – 40in (15 – 100cm)
Flowers:	Late June – August
Sowing:	Sow seeds in late Spring where intended to flower, thin if necessary. Plant in Autumn or Spring. Divide plants in either Autumn or Spring.
Position:	Dry, chalky soil, well-drained and in sunny position. Seeds can be sown in ordinary garden soil.
Note:	Food plant of Elephant Hawk Moth.

Milkwort

Polygala vulgaris

Cross Flower, Fairy Soap, Four Sisters, Gang Flower, Mother Mary's Milk, Procession Flower, Rogation Flower, Shepherd's Thyme.

Gerard, the Elizabethan surgeon and horticulturist, wrote that the Milkwort 'Doth flourish in the Crosse or Gang Week, or Rogation week'. Garlands of Milkwort were made for girls to wear in the processions leading up to Ascension Day. It is fairly certain, however, that these festivities date from a far older festival celebrated by the Romans, called 'Ambervalia', and the Milkwort was once named *Ambervalia flos*.

The generic name stems from the Greek *poly*, meaning 'much' and *gala*, 'milk'. Country folk believed that it ensured greater milk yields in their cattle, but this subsequently came to refer more to nursing mothers.

These are rather unusual but pretty plants with interesting flowers which can be white, blue, mauve or even pink, which possibly led to the Irish name for the plant of 'Four Sisters'.

They are of limited culinary importance although the leaves and flowers can be eaten as a vegetable or in soups, but they are rather bitter to the palate and it is best cultivated as an ornamental plant. In the eastern United States a similar Milkwort plant, *senega* or *seneca snakeroot* which has white flowers, is used as an expectorant. This plant's specific name is taken from the Indian tribe, Senega.

Milkwort

Perennial	
Size:	Up to 5in (12.5 cm)
Flowers:	May – September
Sowing:	Sow seeds in May/June in a reserve border and thin to about 6in (15cm) apart. When plants large enough to handle (about September) transfer to flowering position. Divide in Autumn.
Position:	Good garden soil. Prefers chalky soil, and sunny position.

Buttercup

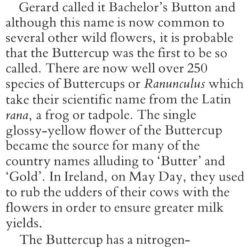

Ranunculus acris

Butter-and-Cheese, Butterchurn, Crazy Weed, Cuckoo Buds, Dellcup, Fairies Basins, Gildcup, King's Clover, Teacups, Yellow Creams.

Everyone is familiar with Buttercups, particularly when they are seen *en masse* in meadowland in late Spring. Culpeper summed them up very well, 'Many are the names this furious biting Herb hath obtained. They grow common everywhere. Unless you run your Head into a Hedge, you cannot but see them as you walk'. Yet the actual common name of 'Buttercup' only came into general use in the seventeenth century. Before then it had been known under a variety of different names, Crowfoot and Butter-flower among many others.

Gerard called it Bachelor's Button and although this name is now common to several other wild flowers, it is probable that the Buttercup was the first to be so called. There are now well over 250 species of Buttercups or *Ranunculus* which take their scientific name from the Latin *rana*, a frog or tadpole. The single glossy-yellow flower of the Buttercup became the source for many of the country names alluding to 'Butter' and 'Gold'. In Ireland, on May Day, they used to rub the udders of their cows with the flowers in order to ensure greater milk yields.

The Buttercup has a nitrogen-poisoning quality and it is best not to let it near the vegetable plot. It can stunt the growth of any peas or beans. Small animals have fallen foul of the plant and it is not wise to experiment with it; advice should be sought if considering its homeopathic uses, although it was used once for the alleviation of skin problems and arthritis.

Meadow Buttercup

Perennial	
Size:	6 – 30in (15 – 75cm)
Flowers:	June – July
Sowing:	Sow seeds in open ground in either Autumn or Spring, where intended to flower. Plants can be set out in flowering positions anytime during the Winter. Division not necessary until the clump becomes too overcrowded.
Position:	Full sun in almost any soil as they are extremely hardy, but you should keep the ground moist.
Note:	Very resistant to heat, cold and diseases.

Field Madder

Sherardia arvensis

Catchweed, Evergreen Cliver.

The Field Madder which Edith Holden illustrated differs from the Cultivated Madder, as it does not have the same dyeing properties. The roots of the Field Madder do not give the same intense reddish dye as the true Madder, yet it has been used for research purposes.

Field Madder stains the bones of birds and animals which feed upon it and this fact is used by physiologists to record bone growth in animals.

The true Madder, *Rubia tinctorum*, has been used throughout history for its dye. Cloth found in Egyptian burial chambers had been dyed with Madder and Herodotus recorded that the women of Libya also used the dye for their clothing. Nowadays synthetic substances have replaced the Madder and reduced the need for any intensive cultivation, although it is still popular with artists and craftsmen because of the reddish dye produced, it can also be combined with Weld to give an intense orange dye.

In medicine Madder has been used as a cure for both dropsy and palsy and occasionally as a form of 'wound' herb. In Wales it was made into a decoction to be drunk both in the evening and the following morning by those suffering wounds. The healing process was helped if a red cabbage leaf was also applied, externally, to the affected place.

Perennial	
Size:	4 – 18in (10 – 45cm)
Flowers:	May – October
Sowing:	Sow the seeds in open ground in intended flowering position in Spring or Autumn. The seeds need to be subjected to cold to break down the husk and can be sanded down or kept in a refrigerator before sowing. Divide in either Spring or Autumn.
Position:	Either full sun or even partial shade. Any ordinary rich garden soil.

Blue Field Madder

Ox-Eye Daisy

(Chrysanthemum leuchanthemum)
Leucanthemum vulgare

*Bull Daisy, Devil's Daisy, Dutch Morgan,
Fair-Maids-of-France, Horse Gowlan,
Margaret, Moon Daisy, Open Star, Rising
Sun, White Golds.*

Ox-eye Daisy

Apart from the rather sinister local name of Devil's Daisy, the Ox-eye Daisy was much sought after by both herbalists and lovers. Each flower of the Ox-eye Daisy lent itself admirably to the old country custom for love divination, whereby plucking out each petal to the chant of 'she loves me, loves me not' would foretell either happiness or more hard work.

Other country names, 'Fair-Maids-of-France' and 'Marguerite', are a reference to Margaret of Anjou the fifteen-year-old princess who chose a spray of three Ox-eye Daisies as embroidered decoration on her robes for her marriage to Henry IV in 1445.

The flowers are in bloom during mid-Summer and have been ascribed as one of the plants for the Feast of St John on 24th June.

It falls under the dominion of Venus and is therefore considered excellent for wounds in the breast, for relieving bruises and can be taken internally for catarrh. Pechey advocated that the whole herb, stalks, flowers and leaves could be boiled in water and taken for asthma and difficulty in breathing. The young leaves are eaten in salads, but sparingly, and wine can be made from the flowers in the same manner as Dandelion wine.

Perennial
Size:	12 – 24in (30 – 60cm)
Flowers:	June – August
Sowing:	Sow direct into ordinary garden soil in Spring. Or into trays of good soil in cold frame in the Spring and plant in flowering position in Autumn. Divide in Autumn.
Position:	Good garden soil in full sun.

Tormentil

Potentilla erecta

Blood Root, Five-Finger-Blossom, Flesh and Blood, Shepherd's Knot, Snake's Head, Tormenting Root.

An attractive little plant growing no more than a few inches high and one of the *Potentilla* genus, which also includes the Cinquefoils, and which were considered 'potent' in a medical sense.

The Tormentil differs from the Creeping Cinquefoil in that it usually has four petals for each flower, rather than the Cinquefoils five or occasionally six. The Tormentil also bears three slightly more prominent but slender leaves, whilst the Cinquefoil has five leaves with rounded edges.

Although *tormentilla*, in Medieval Latin, means agony or torment, the plant was so named for the relief that it gave, rather than for the agony it imparted, and was frequently used as a cure for toothache.

Herbalists have recommended that chewing the rhizome would also alleviate mouth ulcers and other oral complaints.

A red dye can be extracted from the roots of *Potentilla erecta* which was used as a substitute for oak bark in the tanning industry and which fishermen in Scotland used to dye their nets. This red dye led many to call the plant 'Blood Root' and in the Doctrine of Signatures this bloodlike dye was considered capable of staunching the blood flow, an action which could be greatly strengthened if given '… in water wherin hot steele hath been often quenched'.

Perennial	
Size:	3 – 20in (7.5 – 50cm)
Flowers:	May – October
Sowing:	Sow seeds in greenhouse in moist, rich loam in Spring, transfer plants to final flowering position in early Autumn. Plant in Autumn or Spring in flowering position. Divide in either Autumn or Spring.
Position:	Light acid soil in sunny position well-drained or partial shade.
Note:	Do not allow roots to dry out.

Tormentil

Meadow Cranesbill

Geranium pratense

Blue Basins, Blue Warrior, Gipsy, Granny's Bonnets, Loving Andrew.

The large, soft violet flowers of the Meadow Cranesbill have graced many a garden over the centuries together with its darker relative, the Dusky Cranesbill. Even Jefferies in his *Wild Life in the Southern Country* stated that the Meadow Cranesbill should be a garden flower and not 'left to the chance mercy of the scythe'. Both Cranesbills remain in flower longer than many other garden flowers and, consequently, make a fine show.

Although the name for the plant in Germany was *Göttesgnade*, which was freely translated as Grace of God, there is evidence to suggest that this was another Christianization of a far older name. In Scandinavian mythology the Meadow Cranesbill was called *Odin's Grace*, or *Odin's Flower*. There could also be a further connection with Scandinavian mythology, however. In Iceland it was once a practice to extract a blue dye from the plant's roots with which to colour the cloaks that adorned the heroes of the Icelandic sagas. The country name of 'Blue Warriors' may also refer to this practice.

The Dusky Cranesbill, *Geranium phaeum* was probably not a native plant but was introduced to Britain about Roman times. In parts of the North of England the plant is called 'Mourning Widow' due to its darker almost purple flowers, and the associations which that colour has with grief and mourning.

Both of the Cranesbills are vigorous plants which unfortunately distribute their seed widely and which will demand care if they are not to spread outside their designated area in the garden.

Dusky Cranesbill

Perennial	
Size:	12 – 30in (30 – 75cm)
Flowers:	June-September
Sowing:	Sow direct into open ground in March/April or in the Autumn where intended to flower the following year. Divide in Autumn or Spring.
Position:	Ordinary light soil either in sun or partial shade.
Note:	If sowing in Spring, the husk of the seed should be sanded down, to allow seed to germinate more quickly.

Forget-me-Not

Myosotis scorpioides

*Bird's Eye, Bugloss, Love-Me, Mammy
Flower, Robin's Eye, Water Mouse Ear,
Scorpion Grass.*

Nearly everyone knows the legend of
how the Forget-me-Not achieved its
name. A young German knight, walking
by the side of the river with his lady,
stooped to pick the tiny Myosotis flowers
from the riverside. He fell into the river
and barely had time to hand the picked
flowers to his loved-one before being
swept away. However, his final words
were 'vergiss mein nicht'. There are many
such legends regarding the beautiful little
Forget-me-Not. Not least how Adam,
when naming all the flowers in the
Garden of Eden, overlooked the Forget-
me-Not. Yet all these tales have the same
central idea of remembrance which
preceded that association now given to
the Flanders Poppy. Following the battle
of Waterloo the fields were reported to be
carpeted with Forget-me-Nots, which
were believed to represent the fallen.

There seems to be no precise date when
the name entered the English language,
although when Henry of Lancaster was
banished by Richard III he chose the
flower as his symbol and as a reminder to
his followers to remain steadfast.
Shakespeare makes no mention of this or
even the Forget-me-Not, by name, in any
of his works. The Forget-me-Nots (of
which there are several species) have
remained a symbol of love and fond
remembrance since the Middle Ages,
when it was worn as a token of affection.

Under the Doctrine of Signatures it was
believed to be effective against the bite of
the scorpion or any venomous beast,
owing to the shape of the buds which curl
round and resemble a scorpion's tail. A
common name for the plant was
'Scorpion Grass'.

Perennial	
Size:	6 – 12in (15 – 30cm)
Flowers:	May – September
Sowing:	Sow seeds in drills in reserve border in early Summer. When large enough to handle plant out in flowering position in Autumn.
Position:	Any moist, deep, slightly acid soil in sun or partial shade.
Note:	Self-seeding.

Water Forget-me-Not

Dog Rose

Rosa canina

Local Plant names: *Briar, Brimmle, Canker Rose, Dog's Briar, Horse Bramble, Lawyers, Neddy-Grinnel, Rose Briar.*

Local Fruit names: *Cankers, Cat-choops, Dog Berries, Dike Rose, Haws, Hedgie-Pedgie, Pixie Pears.*

The term 'dog' applied to any plant usually implied either lack of smell or a certain inferiority to other plants. In the case of the Dog Rose, however, the name came to us from an early belief among the Greeks that the Wild Rose was a cure for dog bites, and Pliny named the plant *Rosa canina*; a literal translation of this led to the plant being called the Dog Rose. Years ago an extraction of the root was claimed to be a cure for rabies. The Dog Rose is noted for its longevity, and there is a story that a Dog Rose which was planted by Charlemagne in about 850AD still grows in the garden of a convent in Germany.

The Dog Rose was adopted as the symbol of English monarchy during the reign of Henry VIII, and despite something of a preference, more recently, for the design to feature more often the cultivated Rose it was the Wild Dog Rose which was originally chosen. The famous scene in Shakespeare's *Henry VI* when the Houses of Lancaster and York choose their red and white Roses took place in a garden, and the Roses were more likely to have been a cultivated variety than the Wild Rose.

Although the methods for growing the Wild Rose are similar to that for cultivated kinds, *Rosa canina* has proved more beneficial medicinally. The high vitamin C content in the hips make up into a useful syrup for children and during the Second World War a government campaign of hip collection yielded vast quantities of Rosehip syrup, when oranges were scarce. From the leaves a very astringent, but very soothing, tea can be made.

Fruit of the Dog Rose

Perennial	
Size:	up to 12ft (3.6m)
Flowers:	June – July
Note:	Planting Dog Roses is the same as for any climbing garden roses. The Dog Rose makes excellent stock on which to bud garden roses.
Position:	The same soil as used for garden roses. Excellent hedgerow plant.

'For the Rose, ho, the Rose! is the eye of the flowers,
  Is the blush of the meadows that feel themselves fair,
  Is the lightning of beauty that strikes thro' the bowers,
On pale lovers who sit in the glow unaware.
Ho, the Rose breathes of love! ho, the Rose lifts the cup
  To the red lips of Cypris invoked for a guest!
  Ho! the Rose, having curled it's sweet leaves for the world,
  Takes delight in the motion it's petals keep up
            As they laugh to the wind, as it laughs
            from the west!'

E.B.B. Trans from Sappho

Wild Dog Rose

Honeysuckle

Lonicera periclymenum

Bindwood, Eglantine, Honeybind, Irish Vine, Pride-of-the-Evening, Suckle Bush, Trumpet Flower, Withywood, Woodbind.

The heady perfume of the Honeysuckle on Summer evenings is one of the most evocative scents of the countryside.

The generic name comes from a dedication by Linnaeus to the German botanist Adam Lonicer, and the specific name from the Greek *perikleia*, I entwine.

The leaves can appear very early in the year even though the flowers do not appear until June. These flowers grow in pairs on opposite sides of the stem and were taken to symbolise two lovers, and the clinging, twining habit of the stems gave the Honeysuckle romantic associations. There was also a belief that if the Honeysuckle were carried into the home a marriage would surely take place very soon after.

The Honeysuckle was also popular with herbalists and was the means of alleviating several ailments. As early as 77 AD Dioscorides wrote of the effects a drink made from the seeds of Honeysuckle had upon the spleen and the relief of 'wearisomness'. It was more often used to combat headaches, lung infection and asthma. Culpeper advised using the flowers, strewn about the house as being 'No better cure for asthma'.

Honey bees cannot reach the pollen at the deep base of the flowers but the plant is visited by Hawkmoths and, in the New Forest, the rare White Admiral butterfly, one sure indication of having a dormouse in the area is if the bark of the Honeysuckle has been stripped away at the base of the stems.

Honeysuckle

Evergreen
Deciduous shrub, perennial
Size: Up to 20ft (6m)
Flowers: June – August
Growing: Cuttings taken in July can be rooted in sandy soil in pots under glass. When roots are established re-pot and grow on for Spring planting.
Can also be grown from seed sown in greenhouse in February and, if ready, planted either in October or following Spring.
Position: Ordinary soil, well-drained and in a shady situation.

Figwort

Scrophularia nodosa

Brownwort, Carpenter's Square, Cut-finger, Fairies' Beds, Hasty Roger, Poor Man's Salve, Rose Noble, Stinking Roger, Scrofula Plant.

The Figwort is smelly, the whole plant is rather unattractive and the flowers are dull brown and green. Yet the Irish called it the Queen of the Herbs – the Foxglove being the King.

Like the Celandine, the Figwort was considered beneficial in curing the piles as its tuberous roots were the same shape as the ailment. This is another example of the 'signature' of a plant, the likeness of a particular disorder and its possible remedy being illustrated in the shape or colour of certain parts of that plant. The square stem was thought to be further proof of a signature and Figwort was known as 'Carpenter's Square' for the wound-healing effect it might have for careless carpenters.

Known also as the Scrofula Plant, it was efficient in the treatment of the dreaded tubercular disease of the lymphatic glands known as 'King's Evil', and the Figwort is still used today for its effect upon mastitis and conjunctivitis.

There are precious few culinary uses for the plant but the fact that the roots are edible was of great benefit to the troops of Cardinal Richelieu during their defence of La Rochelle in 1628. They survived the siege on a diet made entirely of the Figwort. For their deliverance, and in recognition of the plant, the French named the Figwort 'Herbe de Siège'.

The Figwort is visited by hordes of wasps in the flowering season who pollinate the plant.

Figwort

Perennial	
Size:	30 – 48in (75 – 120cm)
Flowers:	July – October
Sowing:	Sow seeds either in open ground in early Spring or in the Autumn where intended to flower. Propagate by either reseeding or cuttings taken in the Autumn.
Position:	Any good garden soil, in the shade, and with a certain amount of moisture.
Note:	Pollinated by flies and wasps attracted by 'carrion' smell.

Creeping Cinquefoil

Potentilla reptans

Creeping Jenny, Five Finger Blossoms, Five Finger Grass, Golden Blossoms.

The Cinquefoils, all members of the rosaceous genus *Potentilla*, take their common name from the arrangement of the five leaflets. Except for the Tormentil with four petals, all the Cinquefoils have five-petalled yellow flowers.

When people refer to the Cinquefoil they tend not to make any actual distinction between the separate members of the genus and refer most often, to *Potentilla reptans*, the Creeping Cinquefoil.

They were long regarded as full of magic and mystery and believed to possess supernatural powers. As with the Wood Avens and Herb Bennet, the five leaves and five petals symbolised the Five Wounds of Christ, and for this reason it was often represented in church carvings in the Middle Ages and it was considered important to hang bunches of Cinquefoil above the doorway to repel witches from the home. The Cinquefoil was also represented in heraldry from earliest times although in the earlier examples there is virtually no distinction, in shape at least, between the Rose and the Cinquefoil. Cinquefoils put out long runners which take root wherever they touch new ground, rather like the Wild Strawberry.

Culpeper said of the Cinquefoils 'Some hold that one leaf cures a quotidian, three a tertian, and four a quartan ague, and a hundred to one if it be not Dioscorides, for he is full of whimsies'. In this respect a 'quotidian' meant every day, 'tertian' every other day and 'quartan' stood for every third day.

Perennial	
Size:	Up to 4in (10cm)
Flowers:	June – September
Sowing:	Sow seeds in greenhouse or cold frame in March in loamy soil, planting out when large enough to handle in flowering position. Alternatively, sow direct into open ground in early June where intended to flower. Division in March/April. Plant in either Spring or late Autumn.
Position:	Rich well-drained garden soil in partial shade or full sun.
Note:	Reproduces by means of long stems, new roots can be repositioned after cutting away from main stem, or brought on in pots.

Creeping Cinquefoil

Clover

Red Clover: *Trifolium pratense*

Bee Bread, Clover Rose, Honeystalks, King's Crown, Marl Grass, Sleeping Maggie, Sucklings, Sugar-plums.

White Clover: *Trifolium repens*

Baa-lambs, Broad Grass, Curl-Doody, Pussy Foot, Quillet, Sheep's Gowan, White Sookies.

Purple Clover

White or Dutch Clover

Although there is no firm evidence to say precisely which of the trefoiled-patterned plants was the actual one which St Patrick chose to illustrate the Doctrine of the Trinity to the Irish, Clover is a possibility. However, many English poets believed it to be the Wood Sorrel, whilst other sources point to the Lesser Yellow Trefoil, which is more often associated with St Patrick. However, Shamrock in Irish gaelic is *seamrag*, a diminutive of *seamar*, meaning trefoil. What is much more certain is that Clover provided the club symbol on a pack of playing cards, derived from the Latin *clava*, for a club. To find a four-leaf Clover was considered lucky, not just because it was rare, but more because it represented the sign of the Cross and was frequently worn or carried as a lucky mascot against the evil from witches and warlocks.

Clovers are also a very valuable source of honey for beekeepers and in former days children would pick the flowerheads in order to suck out the nectar secreted there. This led to the folk name for the Clover of 'Honeysuckles'.

In many country areas, the Red Clover was employed in the production of a rather potent but delicious Clover Wine and also to make Red Clover tea from the dried flowers infused in boiling water.

Red Clover
Perennial
Size: up to 20in (50cm)
Flowers: May – September

White Clover
Perennial
Size: up to 18in (45cm)
Flowers: June – September

Sowing: Clover will grow easily from seed in any good garden soil. Roots can be divided easily and replanted.

Position: Clovers thrive in soil having a high pH, that is rather limey. But unless intended to feature as a lawn, it should be kept away from that area.

Yellow Iris or Flag

Demoiselle Dragonfly

Yellow Flag

Iris pseudacorus

Dragon Flower, Duck's Bill, Flagger, Leavers, Queen-of-the-Marshes, Sword Flower, Trinity Plant, Water Skegg, Yellow Spear.

Although the Yellow Flag was called 'Water-flag' and 'bastard floure-de-luce' in Gerard's Herbal of 1597 there is certainly evidence to link the *Iris pseudacorus* with the Fleur-de-Lis symbol in heraldry.

The Fleur-de-Lis was adopted as the symbol of Clovis, first King of France. The legend relates that Clovis, King of the Franks, was cut off at a bend in the river near Cologne by a superior force of Goths. Noticing that the Yellow Irises grew far out into the river he reasoned that the water was quite shallow and succeeded in taking his Marovingian army across. In gratitude for his deliverance he took the Yellow Iris as his emblem. The three petals of the Yellow Flag stood for Faith, Wisdom and Valour and during the Crusades it was known as the 'Flower-of-Louis', although this symbol was later outlawed, at the time of the French Revolution.

The common name of Yellow Flag most probably came from a combination of Scandinavian and Middle English names about the fourteenth century. In Denmark it was *flaeg*, and in Middle English *flagge* meant a sword, an allusion to the shape of the leaves.

The Fleur-de-Lis has been used in many connections over the years – even as the North point symbol in cartography. This was devised by the cartographer to the King of Naples, a member of the French royal family.

It was also a special herb of St John's Eve with the power to avert evil and, due to its yellow colouring, an emblem of the month of May and for those whose birthday fell on May 5th.

Apart from a reference of about 1820 to producing a sort of coffee from the seeds, the only other use to which the plant has been put, apart from decoration, was to yield a black dye from the roots which was very like ink. The roots were also powdered and made up into teething rings for babies. However, the rhizome is poisonous and should not be used in the home.

Perennial

Size:	Up to 4ft (122cm)
Flowers:	May – July
Sowing:	Seeds can take about 18 months to germinate. Container-grown plants or propagation by division is more satisfactory. Plant tubers (or divide) in August – October, either at pool side in more than 6in (15cm) water, or in herbaceous border.
Position:	Ordinary soil, deeply dug and with some lime added, if grown in border flower bed. Full sun, but water regularly.
Note:	When dividing from the existing roots cut into sections and ensure an 'eye' with each. New shoots will appear from this if placed in the soil with 'eye' exposed to sun.

Great Burnet

Sanguisorba officinalis

*Bloodwort, Drumsticks, Garden Burnet,
Maiden's Head, Parasol, Red Heads,
Red Knobs.*

Of the two Burnet plants probably the
Salad Burnet *Sanguisorba minor* is better
known, particularly for its culinary
applications. But Great Burnet has been
known for centuries as a great stauncher
of blood. The Doctrine of Signatures
ascribed this quality to the plant from the
colour of the flower heads. These are of a
dark reddish brown, very similar, it was
thought, to the colour of blood.
Burnet was, therefore, a much
sought-after 'wound' herb.
The effect of the plant was
astringent and the dried leaves were
infused and drunk against diarrhoea and
intestinal disorders. Burnet's common
name came from the French *brunette*
meaning brown, another reference
to the flower heads.

Culpeper lauded its praises by stating
that it was 'a most precious Herb, the
continual use of it preserves the body
health and the spirit in vigour'.

Great Burnet

Ragged Robin

Salad Burnet was, as its name suggests,
used for salads and also for cooling
drinks, particularly delicious when added
to Borage. It was also added to beers and
wines as a spice.

Ragged Robin

Lychnis flos-cuculi

Bachelor's Buttons, Billy Buttons, Cock Robin, Cuckoo Flower, Drunkards, Indian Pink, Meadow Spink, Polly Baker, Rough Robin, Shaggy Jacks.

The unmistakable Ragged Robin, growing in mid-Summer in damp meadows and marshland, is related to the Red Campion and even shares some of the same traditional characteristics.

Both are plants associated with the cuckoo, and the picking of either of them was considered unlucky.

The flowers of the Ragged Robin each have five petals which are divided into four segments giving the flower a somewhat 'ragged' appearance accounted for in the common name.

Further similarities with the Campion also exist in the country names for the two flowers. References to robins and cuckoos abound. However, in the case of the Ragged Robin the allusion may be to the popular farce of Robin and Marion, played out for country folk at Pentecostal festivals. The players wore extremely ragged clothes. But this apart, any reference to 'Robin' usually held sinister associations and the belief that the plant belonged to goblins and evil spirits.

There has also been a suggestion that the 'crowflowers' mentioned in Ophelia's garland, in Shakespeare's *Hamlet*, were in fact not Buttercups but Ragged Robin. This belief has been based partly upon Gerard's mention that Ragged Robin was used, as he put it, 'for garlands and crowns, and to deck up gardens'.

Ragged Robin

Perennial
Size: 10–24in (25–60cm)
Flowers: May–August
Sowing: Sow under glass in February. When large enough transplant to cold frame to harden off in trays and plant out end of April. Alternatively sow in reserve bed in early Summer and plant out in September where intended to flower.
Position: Soil can be moist and in shade. Plant thrives on clay in the wild.
Note: Large moths are attracted to the flowers.

Great Burnet

Perennial
Size: 18–36in (45–90cm)
Flowers: June–September
Sowing: Sow seeds in the Spring where intended to flower, thinning to 6in (15cm) apart. Division of the tough root stock in October. Replant in flowering position.
Position: Ordinary garden soil but which does not dry out in the heat of Summer.

Salad Burnet

Perennial
Size: 6–14in (15–35cm)
Flowers: June–August
Sowing: Same sowing instructions as for the Great Burnet.
Position: Any ordinary garden soil. The plant thrives on chalk.

Foxglove

Digitalis purpurea

Bloody Fingers, Bee-catchers, Deadman's Bellows, Dragon's Mouth, Pop-ladders, Snapjack, Ladies Thimbles, Fairy Thimbles, Folk's Glove.

One of the most dramatic of wild flowers, although the exact origins of its name are frequently shrouded in superstition, magic and fairie-lore. The popular traditional name of Folk's Glove (or Fairies Glove) refers to the supposed use made of the bell-like flowers as resting places for fairies, and elves are believed to have invested the flowers with magical properties before fitting them to the paws of foxes, enabling them to sneak 'in magic silence' about their unlawful activities.

However, the name may also have come from the name applied to a musical instrument popular in Anglo Saxon times called *foxes-glien*, bearing a close resemblance to the popular name of Fox's Glove. This consisted of a ring of bells suspended from a hand-held, arched support.

On a more practical level, it was the German botanist Leonhard Fuchs, obviously inspired by local terms for the Foxglove of Ladies Thimbles and Fingers who applied the generic name *Digitalis* to the plant in 1542. The specific name of *purpurea* came from the colour of the flowers.

Whilst early herbalists found little use for the plant, save in the treatment of dropsy, the important medical properties of the Foxglove were more fully appreciated in 1785 by William Withering, who proved that the plant acted upon the heart and was a good diuretic. This led, eventually, to the discovery of the beneficial effect from the extracted drug *digitalin* in the treatment of cardiac disorders. The Foxglove is one of the most poisonous native plants and should *never* be used in preparations in the home. As Culpeper pointed out, 'It is best therefore not to meddle with it, lest the cure end in the churchyard'.

Biennial	
Size:	18 – 60in (45 – 150cm)
Flowers:	June – August
Sowing:	Sow seeds on the surface of reserve bed in May/June, with a little soil to cover. Thin when large enough to 6in (15cm). Plant out in September where intended to flower. 15in (27.5cm) apart. Planting roots will only be really successful if done in Spring.
Position:	Any good garden soil but prefers sandy, siliceous soil. Semi-sun or shade.
Note:	Due to height, plant at the rear of any border. *All parts of the Foxglove are poisonous even when dried.*

Foxglove and
Trailing Rose

White Water Lily

Nymphaea alba

*Bobbins, Can-Dock, Floating Dock, Lady of
the Lake, Swan-amongst-the-Flowers,
Waterblob, Water Rose.*

Whereas the Yellow Water Lily has a
scent not too far removed from the smell
of 'old brandy bottles' the White Water
Lily is scentless. Its brilliant white petals
stand upon smooth, deeply heart–shaped
leaves, which are often red when the plant
is very young.

Despite the fact that the White Water
Lily is a native plant, Shakespeare makes
no mention of it in any of his works,
although, at about that time, it was
referred to as Nenuphar, from the French,
and a derivation of the name for a similar
shaped plant from India known in sanskrit
as *nilotpala*.

It shared the symbolism of the Yellow
Water Lily, being noted for absolute
purity, even to the extent of being
thought to induce chastity in Elizabethan
England. Those with thoughts in other
directions were advised to eat the seeds

Perennial	
Size:	Stems can be very long. Flowers up to 10in (25cm)
Flowers:	June – August
Planting:	Use special containers filled with rich loam and immersed in the pool. Seeds can be sown in similar soil and when large enough transferred to final container. Plant from Spring to Summer. Division in Spring.
Position:	Full sun but will stand partial shade. Rich loam with no chemical additives.
Note:	Propagate by removing eyes and new shoots.

and the rhizome to assuage their 'hunger'.
Yet these are in fact stimulating, rather
than relaxing, and it has subsequently
been found that the plant is good for the
heart and stimulates the spleen.
Dioscorides also recommended it for
dysentery.

White Water Lily

July

The month of July was originally named after Julius Caesar, although the Anglo Saxons called it *haeg-monath* meaning the 'month of hay'.

July is the continuation of high Summer with all the lushness of Summer wild flowers. Bellflowers and the beautifully scented Meadowsweet, the ubiquitous Stinging Nettle and the Rosebay Willow Herb being among the most prominent. But also a time when the smaller Bird's Foot Trefoil and the Eyebright are at their best, and when Vetches garland the hedgerows of country lanes.

In addition to keeping weeds in check and ensuring adequate moisture for established plants during the hot weather, plans should also be made for work in the wild flower garden during the Autumn. Check on the development of seeds sown earlier in the year and which are due for planting out in the next few months. Cuttings can be taken of the Bittersweet and then grown on in pots during the Winter, and seeds of Alkanet should be sown under glass ready for planting out either later in the year in a protected site, or over-wintered in a cool greenhouse for the following Spring.

Devil's Bit Scabious

Succisa pratensis

Angel's Pincushion, Blue Buttons, Devil's Bit, Gentlemen's Buttons, Hog-a-Back, Woolly Hardhead.

The common name of the Devil's Bit Scabious is a perfect illustration of how a legend or, in this case, a folk-tale can be perpetuated in a flower's name.

According to the old story, the Devil quite literally, bit! The Devil's Bit Scabious was so effective a plant medicinally that the Devil became jealous of both its power and its popularity. In an attempt to curb these powers the Devil bit off a goodly section of the root. Fortunately the Devil was unsuccessful in reducing the curative properties of the Scabious, yet the shortened root remained. The Medieval Latin name for the plant was *Morsus diaboli*, freely translated as 'Devil's Bite'. Yet the power of the Devil remained. If anyone should pick the flower of the Scabious, or Devil's Button as it was also called, they stood in danger of being carried off by the Devil.

Culpeper prescribed the plant for numerous ailments including the plague, burns, scalds, wind and, surprisingly, dandruff. Something of a 'cure-all'. In medieval times it was called also the *Scabiosa herba* – the scabies plant – and was used to relieve the intense itching that came with the disease.

The Devil's Bit Scabious is also a very valuable plant for the Marsh Fritillary Butterfly and the Bee-Hawk moth.

Devil's Bit Scabious

Perennial	
Size:	4 – 32in (10 – 80cm)
Flowers:	June – October
Sowing:	Sow seeds either in open ground where intended to flower in March or late Autumn. Plant root cuttings *in situ* in Spring. Divide in late Autumn.
Position:	Requires damp, calcareous soil with partial sun.
Note:	Division need only take place after three/four years.

Eyebright

Euphrasia officinalis

Bird's Eye, Fairy Flax, Peeweets, Rock Rue.

There seems to be nothing exceptional about the exquisite little Eyebright at first sight. Yet the apparently dullish white flowers are as intricately worked as the orchid. They are only about ¼in (6mm) across and consist of two, lipped flowers with a patch of both purple and golden–yellow within. The sixteenth century herbalist William Coles, an advocate of the Doctrine of Signatures, believed that the Eyebright, with its purple and yellow spots and stripes, 'Doth much resemble the diseases of the eye' and the Eyebright has always been utilised for eye disorders. Several country names refer to this healing quality by inference, like 'Bird's Eye', a quality which would be given to the eye after treatment, a name shared with the Germander Speedwell.

The Eyebright's generic name *Euphrasia* is from the Greek, meaning 'to gladden' and *euphrasia* led to the other name by which the Eyebright is most commonly known – 'Euphrasy'.

As the poet Spenser wrote:

Yet euphrasie may not be left unsung,
That gives dim eyes to wander leagues
    around.

In addition to the cure for afflicted eyes Culpeper also included the cure of both a weak brain and memory. But this is a little exceptional. Generally it was used for coughs and sore throats as an infusion had rather bitter and astringent qualities.

The Eyebright is also a valuable bee plant.

Common Eyebright

Hardy Annual	
Size:	3 – 12in (7.5 – 30cm)
Flowers:	May – September
Sowing:	The seeds can be sown in open ground in March/ April where intended to flower. Thin young plants to 3in (7.5cm). But a better method is to sow in containers in Autumn and leave outside to be exposed to Winter cold. Then plant out in Spring.
Position:	Grows well on grassy banks and uncultivated ground. Moderate soil. Sun and part shade.
Note:	Self-sown seeds once established. Forms a large shrub in sheltered sites.

Sneezewort and Yarrow

The Sneezewort and the Yarrow are two distinct plants, both cousins of the Daisy. The Sneezewort is a tall slender perennial looking not unlike the Yarrow but having slender saw-toothed leaves and less flowers per flower-head, although these flowers are slightly larger than the flowers of the Yarrow.

Sneezewort

Achillea ptarmica

Goose Tongue, Old Man's Pepperbox.

The Sneezewort achieved its name from the very fact that the powder from it can make one sneeze . As William Turner put it 'the flowers make one sneeze – exceedingly'.

Despite the fact that the Sneezewort was probably a native plant, the first botanical record of the plant was by Gerard in the sixteenth century.

It was used in the Middle Ages for the relief of toothache and the very same qualities which made one sneeze were referred to by Culpeper. He recommended the powder from Sneezewort in order to clear the head. It was also a particularly popular plant for inclusion in the bouquets of young brides. This was due less to its decorative qualities than to the belief that it ensured many years of good fortune during the marriage.

Achillea ptarmica is an easy plant to grow in the garden, and, once established will continue for years.

Sneezewort	
Perennial	
Size:	12 – 24in (30 – 60cm)
Flowers:	July – August
Sowing:	Sow seeds April – June in seedbed, thin out when large enough to 12in (30cm). Plant out in Autumn where intended to flower.
Position:	Border plant, well-drained soil in sunny position.
Note:	Flowers may be cut, while in season, for decoration and also dried for Winter decoration.

Yarrow	
Perennial	
Size:	8 – 20in (20 – 50cm)
Flowers:	June – August
Sowing:	Sow seeds April–June in seedbed, thin out when large enough to 12in (30cm).
Position:	Border plant, well-drained soil in sunny position.
Note:	Yarrow plants may be placed closer together than Sneezewort, 15in (38cm).

Yarrow

Achillea millefolium

Yarrow

Bunch o'Daisies, Carpenter's Herb, Green Arrow, Knight's Balm, Nose Bleed, Old Man's Mustard, Thousand Leaf, Yarroway.

The Yarrow is, nowadays, slightly better known than the Sneezewort. There is a legend that the plant was first used by Achilles, the Greek hero of the Trojan War. He received guidance from Chiron when he sought a plant suitable for healing the wounds of his soldiers. Both Yarrow and Sneezewort took *Achillea* as their generic names. However the property of healing wounds applies more to the Yarrow than the Sneezewort.

In Anglo-Saxon times it was regarded as a powerful 'wound' herb, particularly if the wounds had been caused by 'iron'. Several country names refer to this quality, Knight's Balm, Woundwort, Staunchweed and Carpenter's Herb. This last, from the French *herbe aux charpentier*, refers to the cuts and wounds collected when wood-working.

The Yarrow was further considered effective against evil powers and in France was one of the famous herbs of St John, which were ceremoniously smoked in the bonfires lit on St John's Eve.

Many of these same plants were also considered to have the power of divination, and a country name of 'Nose Bleed' for the Yarrow, may bear some association with the power of divination. If the flower was sniffed and the nose started to bleed it confirmed a loved one's affection.

Gerard's recommendation was that Yarrow cured migraine, by causing the nose to bleed.

St John's Wort

Hypericum perforatum

Amber, Balm of the Warrior's Wound, Penny John, Rosin Rose, Touch-and-Heal, Mary's Ladder.

The perforated St John's Wort is found growing in situations which are drier and more open than those prefered by its relation the Square-stemmed St John's Wort, *Hypericum tetrapterum*. Perforated St John's Wort has slightly larger flowers and the petals contain more black markings around their edges.

Named after St John, this plant seems almost to personify the medieval interest in plants, the Doctrine of Signatures, magic and divination.

It was believed that the blood of St John was contained in the sap from the plant and would act as a healing agent, and the plant was thought particularly effective in combating evil and driving away persistent spirits. It was hung over the doorways of houses, cattle sheds and stables. The powers of the plant could be greatly increased if it were held within the smoke rising from the bonfires on St John's Eve, June 23rd. However, it was required that the St John's Wort to be used for the ceremony had to be picked in a very particular way. The plant must still retain dew when picked, and should be collected before sunrise on June 23rd. Finally, the plant must be found by accident, and not by design.

If these instructions were followed then good fortune would be yours. The French expression *avoir toutes les herbes de St Jean* meant being ready for anything.

An infusion of the flowers, taken over a long period, were said to be an excellent cure for melancholy and general malaise. But here again, the gathering of the plant had to take place only on a Friday within the hour of Jupiter, and the plant should be 'worn for about a week', presumably before infusing.

St John's Wort

Perennial
Size:	12 – 28in (30 – 70cm)
Flowers:	June – September
Sowing:	In cool greenhouse in Feb/March in soil-based compost. Or outdoors in April in flowering position, later thinned to 3in (7.5cm) apart. Division in early Spring.
Position:	Semi-sun and fairly damp soil. Best in sandy, non-calcareous soil.
Note:	St John's Wort is almost scentless.

Meadowsweet

Perennial
Size:	24 – 48in (60 – 120cm)
Flowers:	June – August
Sowing:	Sow in open ground where intended to flower, allowing 6in (15cm) spacing. Thin when established. Division in Spring.
Position:	Moist, rich soil and best if close to a poolside in full sun or in partial shade.

Meadowsweet
or
Queen of the Meadow

Small Upright
St John's Wort

Meadowsweet

Filipendula ulmaria

Bittersweet, Goat's Beard, Kiss-me-Quick, Meadow Queen, Meadwort, Queen of the Meadow, Summer's Farewell, Sweet Hay, Tea Flower.

In Elizabethan England, when houses were not so free of odours as they are now, Meadowsweet was employed to freshen the air. The very fragrant flower heads were combined with other flowers such as Honeysuckle to improve the atmosphere not only in lowly houses and churches but also at Court. The Meadowsweet was a favourite of Elizabeth I.

But the fragrant qualities it possessed were not confined to the home. In the *Mabinogian*, Math, the son of Mathonway went out into the fields and fashioned a wife from the Meadowsweet plant. In Ireland they used to scour out old milk churns with the flowers of Meadowsweet and, according to Culpeper, the leaves could be added to a glass of claret to give it an extra relish. Indeed it was the connection with drink which most probably gave the Meadowsweet its name, rather than the simple fact that it grew in the meadows and was sweet smelling. It was used to flavour the fermented honey drink of Anglo-Saxon times, *mede*, or *mead*.

Meadowsweet also contained many medicinal properties which were effective against malaria and the fluxes. Even today it is used as an infusion for colds and influenza.

Stinging Nettle

Urtica dioica

Devil's Leaf, Devil's Apron, Hidgy-Pidgy,
Jenny Nettle, Naughty Man's Plaything,
Tanging Nettle.

Considered always to be the sign of a neglected garden the Stinging Nettle does actually indicate that the ground

Stinging Nettle

thereabouts is rich in nitrogen, and these Nettles are a staple food plant of the Peacock butterfly and its spiky dark caterpillars.

Cloth made from the Stinging Nettle has been used for centuries. Very popular in Scotland, Nettle cloth was still being made right up to the turn of the present century for tablecloths, linen and clothing. The oldest record, however, was of a Danish burial of the Late Bronze Age where the body was wrapped in a vestment of Nettle cloth. It was also the Danes who believed that the Stinging Nettle would only grow on ground where innocent blood had been shed.

But Stinging Nettles have also had their culinary uses. Nowadays the young shoots can be eaten as a vegetable, but in the past a much wider use was made of them. Nettle soup, Nettle pudding and even Nettle porridge were once popular, presumably among the poorer folk, although Samuel Pepys noted – with almost a note of surprise – that in 1661 'we did eat of some nettle porridge … and it was good'.

Stinging Nettles can also be used for Nettle beer and if that does not allay the stinging sensation, a decoction of the plant made into a salve can be beneficial against Nettle rash.

Perennial	
Size:	Up to 60in (152cm)
Flowers:	May – September
Planting:	If you do not have Stinging Nettles in the garden already then, from those close by, cut out a section of root and replant in any moderate garden soil where required to grow.
Note:	Difficult to restrict.

Rosebay Willow Herb

Epilobium augustifolium

*Blood Vine, Cat's Eyes, Fireweed, Flowering
Withy, French Willow, Ranting Willow,
Wild Snapdragon.*

The Rosebay Willow Herb is familiar
both in flower and when the seeds are
finally pulled from the plant by the
passing breeze. These 'sugar-stealers' as
they were known, can fill the air in the
Autumn carrying the seeds to even more
patches of waste ground. For it is
especially in ground made available after
habitation, and particularly after burning,
that the plant appears to thrive.

   Called 'blitz weed' after the Second
World War, the Rosebay Willow Herb
was one of the first plants to establish
itself after the bombing and fire damage in
built-up areas.

   Yet in Victorian England the plant was
often cultivated as a garden ornamental.
Gerard recorded that the Rosebay Willow
Herb was 'very goodly to behold, for the
decking up of the houses and gardens'.

Rosebay
Willow Herb

Perennial	
Size:	Up to 48in (120cm)
Flowers:	June – September
Sowing:	Sow seeds in open ground in Autumn or early Spring where intended to flower. Divide the plant in the Autumn transferring to similar rich moist soil.
Position:	Sun or part shade in ordinary garden soil.
Note:	Plant spreads by seeds and invasive underground root system and can be difficult to control.

Rosebay Willow Herb was once used to
cure whooping-cough in young children
but apart from this, very little medicinal
use has been made of the plant.

   It is, however, a valuable nectar plant
and farmers around Seattle in North
America make an exceptionally fine
honey from the Rosebay Willow Herb,
called, appropriately, 'Fireweed Honey'.

Heather

Calluna vulgaris

Ling: *Bazzom, Black Ling, Dog Heather, Mountain Mist.*
Cross-leaved Heath: *Bell Heath, Broom, Crow Ling, Father-of-Heath, Wire Ling.*

There is a legend that when Kenneth, called the Conqueror, was warring against the Picts in the hope of converting them to Christianity many savage skirmishes took place and so much Pictish blood was spilt on the ground that those plants covered with the 'heathen' blood became known as Heather. But, more practically, the name Heather appears to come from the fourteenth century when it appears as a form of the word for 'heath'.

This stubby, evergreen shrub was extremely popular in the past for a variety of uses. It could be made up into brushes for sweeping out the house, thatching for the roof, the stems could be made into baskets and, most important of all, it could be used as fuel. It was from this last practice that the Anglo Saxon word 'lig', for fire, developed into the alternative name for Heather of *Ling*. A traditional beverage called heath-ale was brewed from the flowers of the Heather, although some have suggested that the part taken

by Heather was to add flavouring rather than being the sole intoxicant. Heather also provides a valuable crop for sheep and because the Heather is pollinated by bees it also supplies a delightful, clear honey.

Cross-leaved Heath *Erica tetralix*, varies from Ling by growing in damper areas and the leaves and flowers are of slightly different configurations. The leaves of Cross-leaved Heath come in sets of four spaced up the main stem while those of the Ling are contained on the many branched stems and are stalkless. The flowers of Cross-leaved Heath resemble the bell-like flowers of Bell Heather *Erica cinerea*.

Heather or Ling

Fine-Leaved Heath

Ling	
Small evergreen shrub	
Size:	8 – 26in (20 – 65cm)
Flowers:	July – September
Planting:	Plant cuttings or container-grown plants in Autumn or Spring. Propagation from cuttings is the most successful, taking cuttings in middle to late Summer. Bring on under glass in peaty soil and plant out in Autumn, or following Spring. Propagation by layering can be done in Spring.
Position:	Ling: Good well-drained, lime-free soil in open sun. Cross-leaved Heath: Well-drained but moist garden soil, lime-free with some leaf mould.

Bird's Foot Trefoil

Lotus corniculatus

Butter and Eggs, Crow Toes, Devil's Claws,
God-Almighty's-Thumb-and-Fingers,
Lady's Cushions, Love Entangled,
Old Woman's Toenails, Rosy Morn,
Tom Thumb Honeysuckles.

The many references among country names for the Bird's Foot Trefoil and its likeness to 'toes' and 'claws', together with the trefoil pattern of the leaves, very accurately describe this attractive little plant. The slender pods, which turn black and curl slightly at the ends later in the year, look remarkably like the claw feet of certain birds. This bird-like similarity is also evident in the shape of the golden-yellow flowers tinted with patches of red.

Both the generic and specific names speak of this unusual shape. *Lotus* referring to the flower shape and *corniculatus* meaning 'horned' in Greek.

Yet the Lesser Bird's Foot Trefoil is a plant with certain mystical associations as well. It was thought to belong to Tom Thumb, the godchild of the Queen of the Fairies and King Arthur's dwarf.

Bird's Foot Trefoil was held in high regard by certain writers and poets, not least Jefferies who referred to it in *The Open Air* as being the 'Very embodiment of sunshine and summer'.

An abundant and attractive plant in the wild which will grow well in the garden, possibly along with its larger relation the Greater Bird's Foot Trefoil, *Lotus uliginosus*.

Perennial	
Size:	4 – 15in (10 – 37.5cm)
Flowers:	Late May – September
Sowing:	Sow seeds in open ground in March where intended to flower.
	Plant in either Autumn or Spring in flowering position.
	Divide at planting time.
Position:	Chalky and sandy soils. Full sun or part shade.
Note:	Spreads quickly if not restricted by stones or wall.

Lesser Bird's Foot Trefoil
Lady's Slipper
or Lady's Finger and Thumbs

Vetch

The Vetches have received somewhat scant attention over the years, both in medicine and literature. There are numerous members of this genus, some of which have not.had too happy a relationship with farmers, particularly the Hairy Tare *Vicia hirsuta*, which effectively twined its way around growing crops causing numerous problems at harvest time.

Yet in the wild there are few prettier sights than the Vetches with their many coloured flowers in country lanes and straggling over and around hedgerows.

Meadow Vetchling

Meadow Vetchling

Lathyrus pratensis

Angle Berry, Lady's Slipper, Meadow Pea, Mouse Pea, Old Granny's Slipper-Sloppers, Tom Thumb, Yellow Thatch.

Introduced by farmers many years ago as a valuable fodder crop, and because it had the property of introducing much needed nitrogen into the soil.

The Meadow Vetchling is a member of the genus *Lathyrus* which also includes the Sweet Pea, and it resembles the Sweet Pea with its creeping rootstock, angular stems and seed pods.

Although Culpeper makes no mention of the Vetchling it has been suggested that the Greek generic names – *la* meaning 'very' and *thouros* standing for 'impetuous' – relate to certain aphrodisiac properties.

Purple Tufted Vetch

Tufted Vetch

Blue Tan Fitch, Cat Peas, Goose and Ganders, Tare-Fitch, Tine Grass, Wild Tare.

It has been some time now since the Tufted Vetch was a popular addition to gardens and deliberately grown in out of the way areas. *Vicia cracca* is the largest of the wild Vetches and can extend for many feet through hedgerows with its pretty purple-blue flowers. A member of the pea family, it climbs by means of its curling tendrils which grasp any other vegetation in the vicinity.

Tufted Vetch
Perennial

Size:	24–96in (60–240cm)
Flowers:	June – August
Sowing:	Sow seeds in Spring or Autumn in open ground where intended to flower. Propagate by cuttings taken in late Summer or by division in Autumn.
Position:	Calcareous soil, full sun or partial shade.

Meadow Vetchling
Perennial

Size:	12–50in (30–125cm)
Flowers:	May – August
Sowing:	Sow seeds in open ground in Spring, keeping well watered, in position where intended to flower. Propagation by division in early Spring.
Position:	Ordinary soil in either full sun or shade but close to plants suitable for the Vetchling to cling to.
Note:	Valuable nectar plant.

Nipplewort and Hawkweed

Lapsana communis and *Hieracium pilosella*

Bolgan Leaves, Carpenter's Apron, Dockorenes, Hasty Roger, Hasty Sargeant, Jack-in-a-Bush, Swine Cress.

Considering the formation of the flower buds it is not surprising that this slender erect plant became known as the Nipplewort.

John Parkinson first translated into English a name previously used by the Prussian apothecaries. It was known by them as *papillaris* because 'it was goode to heale the ulcers of the nipples of women's breasts'.

The Nipplewort has several flower heads carrying bright yellow flowers arising from a much-branched, hollow stem. These flowers tend to close at the advent of bad weather and in the evening. The young shoots can be collected, before flowering, and used in salads and omelettes, or treated as a vegetable and eaten much like Spinach.

The flowers of the Nipplewort are not unlike those of the Hawkweed. Both plants are members of the Daisy family. Yet the Nipplewort is not a wise consideration for the wild flower garden. The Mouse-ear Hawkweed, *Hieracium pilosella*, is a far better prospect than the Nipplewort and most other Hawkweeds. It resembles in certain ways, a smaller version of the Dandelion.

It would be wise though to confine it to a 'forgotten' corner of the garden as it can spread alarmingly – though not as badly as the other Hawkweeds – and it can be eradicated more easily.

Mouse-ear Hawkweed	
Perennial	
Size:	5 – 18in (15 – 45cm)
Flowers:	June – October
Sowing:	Sow seeds in flowering position in Spring in open ground. Division and replanting in Spring or Autumn.
Position:	Any ordinary soil but away from most other plants. Full sun or part shade.

Common Nipplewort

Bittersweet

Solanum dulcamara

Felon Wood, Fool's Cap, Granny's-Night-Cap, Mad Dog Berries, Poison Flower, Robin-run-the-Hedge, Snakeberry, Witchflower.

The Bittersweet, more popularly called the Woody Nightshade, is related to the Deadly Nightshade but with not quite the same deadly qualities. None the less it is certainly not wise to experiment with Woody Nightshade as its poison is only slightly less deadly. It may not cause immediate death but will severely upset the stomach. A very apt description of the Bittersweet came from Gerard: 'The flowers be small and somewhat clustered together, consisting of five little leaves a peece, of a perfect blewe colour with a certain pricke or yellow pointell in the middle'. The five leaves he referred to are, in fact, the five flame-shaped petals.

Perhaps it is better to employ the Bittersweet as it was often used in the past – to ward off the evil influences of witches. The popular way of doing this was to make a garland of the Bittersweet and place it around the neck of unproductive and infirm pigs and horses – and man – as it was considered effective against dizziness of the head and vertigo. As Culpeper wrote 'It is good to remove witchcraft both in man and beast'.

William Turner was the first to introduce the name Bittersweet into the English language when he translated the Latin name *Amora dulcis*.

Perennial climber	
Size:	Up to about 8ft (210cm)
Flowers:	June – September
Sowing:	It can be grown direct in open ground in Spring but better results come from sowing in individual pots in Spring or Summer and over-winter in a cool greenhouse before planting out the following Spring. Cuttings can also be taken from existing wild plants.
Position:	Hedgerows or against walls. Moist soil and keep well watered for the first two seasons.

Bittersweet

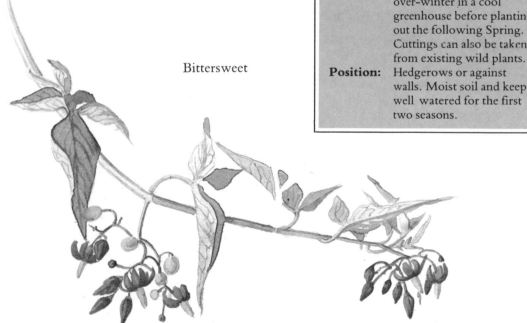

Bindweed

Convolvulus arvensis

*Bear Bind, Bell Bind, Billy Clipper,
Cornbind, Devil's Guts, Fairies' Winecups,
Kettle Smock, Rope Bind, Withywind.*

This straggling, determined perennial is not the wisest of plants to introduce into the garden, yet, depending on the terrain and situation, particularly if there are awkward areas unsuitable for other plants, there could be a case for growing it. But beware, the roots rob the soil and it will easily strangle other plants nearby.

The tips of the stems complete one full circle, anti-clockwise in under two hours, and the roots can be found several feet underground. Otherwise known as Field Bindweed, the generic name comes from the Latin *con-volvo*, 'I wind about' or 'entangle', and the Old English name of *bere* refers to the way in which it wound itself around Barley and was such a nuisance when the crops were gathered.

Yet it is not as actively insidious as the Greater Bindweed, *Calystegia sepium*, also called 'Bellbine', which has large white flowers and is scentless, unlike the Bindweed which attracts many scent-seeking insects.

The Bindweed is certainly vigorous but imparts much of the true feeling of the countryside into the garden so that, if the right area is available, it can be introduced.

Small Bindweed

Perennial	
Size:	8 – 30in (20 – 76cm)
Flowers:	June – September
Sowing:	Sow seeds in moderately warm greenhouse in March, at temperature of 60–65°, prick off young shoots into pots and grow in cold frame until May. Plant out where intended to flower about 12in (30cm) apart. Or sow direct in open ground in Spring, thinning young seedlings.
Position:	Ordinary garden soil, light and warm. Sunny position. Used to cover fences.
Note:	Creeping root system.

Bellflower

Campanula trachelium

Blue Foxglove, Canterbury Bells, Coventry Bells, Throatwort, Our Lady's Thimbles.

Ever since Tudor times the Bellflowers have been firm favourites in the cottage garden, although the true 'Canterbury Bells' have become less popular in recent years, rather losing place to the many other, improved, cultivated Bellflowers now available to the gardener.

It is now more common to find *Campanula persicifolia*, the Peach-leaved Bellflower in modern gardens, which is also quite widely naturalised in various places. The Nettle-leaved Bellflower, *Campanula trachelium*, was originally known as the 'Canterbury Bell'. It took its name from the early botanists, and in particular Gerard, after so many of the flowers were found growing in the countryside close to the city of Canterbury. *Campanula* in Latin meant a 'bell' and there has been an alternative suggestion for the derivation of the term

'Canterbury Bells'. They were thought to resemble the bells hanging from the harnesses of the horses ridden by pilgrims on their way to the shrine of St Thomas á Becket at Canterbury.

Under the Doctrine of Signatures the Bellflower was suggested as a possible cure for diseases of the throat such as tonsillitis, as the shape of the flowers duplicated the shape of the affected area.

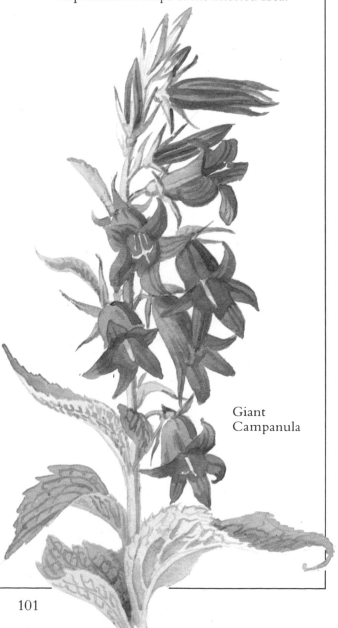

Giant Campanula

Perennial	
Size:	15 – 40in (37.5 – 100cm)
Flowers:	July – September
Sowing:	Sow seeds in open ground in either Autumn or Spring where intended to flower. Planting in either Spring or Autumn. Division at planting times.
Position:	Ordinary garden soil, particularly chalky. Well-drained and with full sun or partial shade.
Note:	Once established the roots can become invasive.

Agrimony

Agrimonia eupatoria

Aaron's Rod, Church Steeples, Cockleburr, Fairy's Wand, Lemonade, Money-in-both-Pockets, Sweethearts.

The spike of small yellow five-petalled flowers of the Agrimony may often be found at the edges of fields and meadows between June and August. This seemingly insignificant plant has, over the years, been considered as very powerful in medicine and magic.

It was one of the fifty-seven herbs mentioned in the Anglo-Saxon Holy Salve and referred to as powerful in combating evil spirits. It was considered to be one of the few herbs capable of being used for various ailments entirely on its own – a 'simple' – rather than one that required combining with other herbs to produce an effect.

Its introduction to medicine can be ascribed to Mithradates Eupator, the King of Pontus during the first century BC, and the plant still bears evidence of this in the scientific name. *Agrimonia* was derived from the Greek *agremone* which stood for a 'cataract' of the eye, implying that the plant might be related to spots or cataracts in the eye, yet there is no real evidence of it having been used for such a treatment. More often it was taken as a general tonic or, as Dioscorides recommended, as part of a cure for snake bites and dysentery.

Agrimonia eupatoria is very similar in looks to the Fragrant Agrimony, *Agrimonia odorata* although that plant is taller and the leaves and flowers larger. Both species of Agrimony were once used to make a country beer which was known, in Somerset at least, as 'Lemonade'.

Common Agrimony

Perennial	
Size:	12 – 36in (30cm – 90cm)
Flowers:	June – August
Sowing:	Sow seeds in either Spring or Autumn where intended to flower. Propagate by root division in the Spring or Autumn.
Position:	Will grow well in any good ordinary soil. Full sun or partial shade.

Common Ragwort

Senicio jacobaea

*Canker Weed, Fairy Horse, James Weed,
Ragged Jack, Sleepy Dose, Stinking Weed,
Summer Farewell, Staggerwort.*

A herb of St James, as its specific name
jacobaea implies, the patron saint of
horses. Yet this allusion to horses was not
confined to the uses of the herb for
veterinary purposes.

It was also sought after by the fairies,
and later, when fairies had fallen from
popularity, it became a favourite means of
transportation for witches. They were
believed to turn the Ragwort into a horse,
enabling them to fly across the skies,
at night.

In America the herb was known as
'Stinking Willie', a name previously used
in Scotland and which may well have
crossed the Atlantic to the New World
carrying Scottish appelation. The Scottish
allusion to the noxious smell of

the plant was a derogatory reference to
William, Duke of Cumberland who
defeated the Scots at the bloody battle
of Culloden.

All species of this genus are poisonous,
but, despite this, Ragwort has been used
medicinally. Culpeper claimed that a
decoction of Ragwort was good for
mouth ulcers and for external swellings
and sciatica. Modern herbalists employ it
for the same purposes.

It would be well introducing it to the
garden as the dramatic and beautiful
Cinnabar moth and its caterpillars feed
upon the leaves.

Common
Ragwort

Perennial	
Size:	24 – 40in (60 – 100cm)
Flowers:	June – October
Sowing:	Sow in flowering position when seeds are ripe, ready for the following year. Or sow seeds in cool frame to over-winter before planting in position in Spring.
Position:	Sun and well-drained, ordinary garden soil.
Note:	Farmers do not like the Ragwort, so confine it to your own garden. Will withstand extreme heat and cold.

Purple Loosestrife

Lythrum salicaria

*Brian Braw, Emmet's Stalk, Long Purples,
Red Sally, Willow Strife.*

The tall flowering stalks of the Purple
Loosestrife, growing anything up to four
feet tall on river banks, streams and in
marshland, display clusters of purplish-
red six-petalled flowers during Summer.

It takes its name from the Greek *lythron*
meaning 'gore', a reference to the colour
of the flowers, and from *salix*, 'a willow'.

This reference to willows and the
waterside habitat of the plant, quite
obviously influenced the painter Millais.
In his depiction of the death of Ophelia
he incorporates the Purple Loosestrife,
together with several other
flowers of the same habitat.
One of the most popular
local names for *Lythrum salicaria*
was 'Long Purples', but whilst
Shakespeare
refers to them in
the garlands which
Ophelia wore, it is fairly
certain that his reference was to
the Early Purple Orchis rather
than the Purple Loosestrife.

The medicinal effect of the
plant was astringent and was
found to stop bleeding, yet
herbalists were to use it
more often for the eyes and as
a mouth gargle for the quinsey.
Even Sir John Hill in his
Herbal recommended it as
something of a wound herb.

The Purple Loosestrife has never found
much favour as a garden plant, a position
occupied far more by the Yellow
Loosestrife, an unrelated plant, but it is
relatively easy to grow in the wild garden.

Both the Great Hairy Willow Herb and
the Purple Loosestrife attract bees, the
Great Hairy Willow Herb producing large
quantities of nectar.

Purple Loosestrife

Great Hairy Willow Herb

Great Hairy Willow Herb

Epilobium hirsutum

Apple Pie, Cherry Pie, Codlins-and-Cream,
Currant Dumpling, Gooseberry Pudding,
Love Apple, Wild Phlox, Wild Willow.

Taller, statelier and more dramatic than the Rosebay Willow Herb, *Epilobium hirsutum* frequents the edges of streams and fenland throughout Britain. The rosy-red and white flowers which bloom from the end of June until August are rather reminiscent of apple blossom, and whilst early botanists claimed that the plant achieved the local name of 'codlins-and-cream' from the fact that when the leaves were crushed they smelled of apples, it is far more likely that it was the similarity to the apple blossom which was responsible, 'codlin' being a type of apple.

The Hairy Willow Herb, dedicated to St Anthony, can be found throughout Europe from Italy to the Arctic Circle and it was in Lapland and Iceland that a 'tea' was made from the Willow Herb by infusing the dried leaves.

It is surprising that a plant which appeared so impressive and which should have had marked medicinal properties, in fact, bore so few. It was once supposed that it could prevent or stop internal bleeding and stop loose bowels, but these ideas have been discarded recently as this form of treatment can lead to poisoning and convulsions. However, it is possible that a herb called by the ancient Greeks *oinotheras* and used to charm away wild animals, was believed to be the Hairy Willow Herb.

The Great Hairy Willow Herb will also produce large quantities of nectar for bees and is visited by the Elephant Hawkmoth.

Purple Loosestrife	
Perennial	
Size:	20 – 48in (50 – 120cm)
Flowers:	June – August
Sowing:	Sow seeds in a cold frame in April and, when seedlings large enough, prick out into reserve bed for planting in flowering position in the Autumn. Divide in the Spring.
Position:	Full sun in any good, damp garden soil. Herbaceous border plant.
Note:	Self seeding.

Great Hairy Willow Herb	
Perennial	
Size:	36 – 60in (80 – 150cm)
Flowers:	July – August
Sowing:	Sow seeds in open ground in Autumn or Spring where intended to flower. Divide the plants in the Autumn transferring to similar soil.
Position:	Full sun or part shade, in rich moist soil.
Note:	Requires damper soil than the Rosebay Willow Herb.

Toadflax

Linaria vulgaris

Bacon-and-Eggs, Dragon Bushes, Fox-and-Hounds, Lion's Mouth, Pig's Chops, Devil's Head, Weasel Snout.

A very definite distinction exists between Yellow Toadflax and Ivy-Leaved Toadflax. The former resembles the Snapdragon while Ivy-Leaved Toadflax is a sprawling plant not unlike an Ivy, as it grows on walls and in crevices.

Although it flourishes in moist habitats, not unlike the toad, the reference to this amphibian in the name is yet another form of 'dog' prefix in the sense of an inferior plant. The stems look very like Flax, before the actual flowers of Flax arrive, and this caused problems when Flax was gathered.

The flowers of Toadflax are smaller than the Snapdragon and form clusters of yellow flowers tinged with orange. The country name of 'Bacon-and-Eggs' was taken from the colouring of the flowers.

Under the Doctrine of Signatures, Toadflax was considered suitable for the cure of jaundice, yet Culpeper

Yellow Toadflax

Perennial	
Size:	Up to 5in (12.5cm)
Flowers:	June – October
Sowing:	Sow seeds in Spring where intended to flower. Alternatively, sow in Autumn, but protect during hard Winters. Division either in Spring or Autumn.
Position:	Rock garden or border. Light general soil, well-drained. Requires sunny position.

commended it as a diuretic and today it is still used in this capacity, sparingly.

Whilst it may be an attractive plant, it has the nasty habit of spreading very easily by its creeping root system.

Yellow Water Lily

Nymphaea lutea

Blobs, Brandy Bottles, Bull's Eyes,
Butterchurn, Crazy Bet, Frog Lily, Queen-of-
Still-Waters, Water Cups, Water Golland.

The striking Yellow Water Lily differs from the White Water Lily in having smaller flowers standing on a raised stem clear of the water. Each of the seed capsules is shaped like a flask and this feature, together with its slight scent, gave the plant the country name of 'Brandy Bottle': the flowers were credited with the smell of old brandy bottle dregs.

In German folklore it was believed that each Water Lily was a water nymph who changed from female form into the flower each time a stranger passed by, and that an evil or mischievous spirit dwelt beneath the leaves ready to take revenge on anyone picking the Water Lily. It was also thought to be such a symbol of absolute purity that it could be employed to break a love potion which had been employed by someone too amorously inclined toward you.

It may only have been due to the distinctive shape of the flower rather than any idea of purity which led thirteenth century sculptors to use the Water Lily as decoration in so many churches. They appear in Westminster Abbey, Bristol Cathedral and Lincoln. Although of no culinary signficance the rhizome was once steeped in tar, applied to the head to cure baldness, and was thought effective in curing the bite of a mad dog.

Perennial	
Size:	Has very large leaves up to 18in (45cm) diameter. Flowers are small, up to 3in (7.5cm).
Flowers:	June – September
Sowing:	Sow seeds under water at about 6in (15cm) depth. Transplant when larger to greater depth. Alternatively, plant into special containers and immerse in pool.
Position:	In still water without much disturbance. Away from overhanging trees. Soil should be a rich loam, free of chemicals.

Yellow
Water Lily

Plantain

Plantago major

Broad Leaf, Canary Flower, Great Waybrede, Healing Blade, Rat's Tails, Traveller's Foot, Waybread.

Water
Plantain

An extremely tough plant, the Plantains were famous as wound herbs, particularly when applied as a poultice to cuts and bruises. As Culpeper stated, 'there is not any martial disease that it does not cure'.

The nature of the plant probably suggested its great healing abilities. It could be trodden on, repeatedly, and still remain strong. The reason being that the growing process of the Plantain is contained in the lowest section of the plant. It has always been the bane of those gardeners who seek for perfect lawns.

It was another of the several herbs of the Festival of St John and also popular as a love diviner. Young ladies once collected them, placing them beneath their pillows at night in the earnest hope of dreaming of their future husbands.

John Josselyn, in an account of New England in 1672, gave proof that the Plantain had travelled across with the early settlers. The local Indians called the plant 'White Man's Foot' in the belief that wherever he trod Plantains would grow.

The Water Plantain, *Alisma plantago-aquatica*, which Edith Holden illustrated is quite unrelated to the other Plantains except that it has similar leaves and was once used in America to cure rattlesnake bites.

Perennial	
Size:	10 – 30in (25 – 75cm)
Flowers:	June – August
Sowing:	Plantains can be either sown from seed or planted direct into ground at any time of the year. Division in Spring.
Position:	Lime rich soil, sunny or partial shade. Preferably away from lawns.

August

August is considered to be the last full month of Summer and a holiday time in many areas. Yet despite the fact that there are often many warm, sunny days still left to enjoy, there is also a hint that Autumn is knocking at the door. This can be felt particularly in the northern areas when temperatures can drop quite remarkably and winds tend to increase towards the end of the month.

While Loosestrife, Foxgloves and the Vetches are coming to an end some of the prettiest wild flowers are at their best during August; the dramatic and familiar Poppy and the delicate Harebell, the true Bluebell of Scotland.

As with the previous month, check for any invasion of weeds. These can become a real problem if the Summer has tended to be rather wet.

August is a month to enjoy the effort you have put into the wild flower garden and to take a short rest before engaging in tasks scheduled for the Autumn.

Thistles

The Cotton Thistle, *Onopordon acanthium*, was assumed to be the thistle chosen as the emblem of Scotland, bearing the motto 'Nemo me impune lacessit', standing for 'No one irritates me unscathed'. This stemmed directly, so it was thought, from the old legend concerning an invasion by the Danes. The Danish forces came upon the camp of the Scots one night, and thinking to overrun the camp with a surprise attack the Danes advanced stealthily and barefooted. Unfortunately, one of the attackers stepped upon a thistle, and in the ensuing melée the Danes were driven off.

This action was believed to have taken place at either the Battle of Largs or the siege of Stains Castle in the reign of Malcolm I.

An interesting legend, but it was certainly not the Cotton Thistle which was responsible for saving the Scots. Most probably it was the Spear Thistle, *Cirsium vulgare*, which was fairly common in Scotland, whereas the Cotton Thistle is quite rare, and it was not until the reign of James III that the thistle was adopted as the national emblem, with the motto 'In Defence'.

Welted Thistle

Cotton Thistle

Creeping Plume Thistle

Cotton Thistle

Onoporordon acanthium

Oat Thistle, Pig Leaves, Queen Mary's Thistle, Scotch Thistle.

The prickly leaved Cotton Thistle which can grow anything up to seven feet tall, was not without its medicinal properties. As Culpeper put it 'It may hurt your finger, but it will help your body', and he noted that both Pliny and Dioscorides advocated a drink made from both the roots and leaves which would help those with a crick in the neck – although Culpeper considered it little use, in this respect, for those meeting the hangman. The young Cotton Thistle shoots can be boiled in salt water, sautéed in butter and eaten like a vegetable.

Welted Thistle

Carduus acanthoides

Buck Thistle, Queen Anne's Thrissel, Teaser.

Welted Thistles are shorter and somewhat weaker than the Cotton Thistle and, as with the other Thistles, take their name from Thor, Norse God of Thunder. Planting thistles close to the home thus ensured that it would escape being hit by lightning.

One delightful feature of the Welted Thistle is the attraction of the seed heads for the Goldfinch. In France the names for both the Goldfinch and the Thistle are very similar, the French for Goldfinch being *Chardonnet* and, for thistle, *Chardon*.

Creeping Thistle

Cirsium arvense

Also known as the Plume Thistle, *Cirsium arvense* is a handsome, but very troublesome weed. During the flowering season it is frequently surrounded by many butterflies – in particular the Painted Lady – as the mauve-pink flowers exude a rich honey scent. However the plant also has a very invasive root system which does not make it popular with either gardeners or farmers.

Cotton Thistle
Perennial
Size:	18 – 60in (45 – 152cm)
Flowers:	June – September
Sowing:	Sow seeds in reserve border in May or June and thin young plants to 9in (?? 5cm). Plant out in September where intended to flower. Allow 36in (90cm) spacing.
Position:	Medium rich or heavy soil in full sun or part shade.

Welted Thistle
Biennial
Size:	12 – 48in (30 – 120cm)
Flowers:	June – August
Sowing:	Sow in September where intended to flower. Thin to 12in (30cm) apart.
Position:	Medium soil with sun or part shade.

Creeping Thistle
Biennial
Size:	12 – 48in (30 – 120cm)
Flowers:	July – September
Sowing:	Sow seeds in open ground in Spring where intended to flower.
Position:	Any garden soil either in full sun or part shade.

Poppy

Papaver rhoeas

Blind Eyes, Butterfly Ladies, Corn Rose, Headache, Paradise Lily, Popple, Red Huntsman, Red Weed, Thunderbolt.

The name of Poppy was derived from the Latin *papaver* through the French *pavot* and this may possibly point to the introduction of the common Poppy into Britain about the time of the Norman incursion.

The Assyrians called the Poppy the "Daughter of the Field" and it has long had an association with agriculture and crops, the Greeks ascribing it to Aphrodite the goddess of vegetation, and the Romans dedicating it to their goddess of agriculture and motherhood, Ceres. The Romans frequently included the Poppy in sacred rites to the Earth Goddess, considering that it had a beneficial effect upon the growing corn. These Roman festivals were later absorbed and Christianized as the Feast of St John. Although poets, over the years, have associated the Poppy with both productive cornfields and rather poorer uncultivated land – among them Crabbe referring to the Poppy mocking the hope of toil – the flower is still one of the most potent symbols of Summer.

The Red Poppy, which now symbolises remembrance and which has associations with the battlefields of Flanders, has been connected with far older battlefields than those of the First World War. The poet Southey, in his *Pilgrimage to Waterloo,* and some earlier records of the battle of Landen in 1693, refer to the fields of Poppies and other flowers, springing up on the days immediately following the battles:

Low pansies to the sun their purple gave,
And the soft poppy blossom'd on the
  grave

All the Poppy family have narcotic qualities, to varying degrees, and were thought to be instrumental in promoting sleep, hence an old country name of 'Sleepy Head'. Yet it was also assumed that just smelling a Poppy brought on a headache, although Poppies were also reported to cure headaches and migraine.

Picking the flower could bring on a thunderstorm in the same way as picking the White Campion, although in certain parts of France placing Poppies in the rafters of a house ensured that it would not be struck by lightning. During the Second World War the oil extracted from Poppies was used as a substitute for olive oil, which had become scarce.

The seeds, if buried, have been known to remain in the ground for up to a century before germinating when dug up.

Common Red Poppy

Annual	
Size:	8 – 24in (20 – 60cm)
Flowers:	June – September
Sowing:	Sow seeds in Autumn where intended to flower the following year. Thin out, if necessary, in March.
Position:	Full sun, light, well-drained soil. May require watering in extremely hot weather.
Note:	Poppies do not take to transplanting, but are self-seeding.

Grass of Parnassus

Parnassia palustris

White Buttercup, White Liverwort.

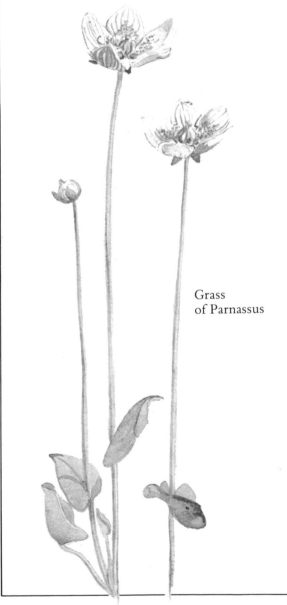

Grass
of Parnassus

The delicate, beautiful Grass of Parnassus is not an actual grass. Its flowers resemble more the Buttercup, even though it is not related to that genus, and an old country name for the flower was White Buttercup.

Mount Parnassus, the holy mountain of Apollo and the Muses north of Delphi appears to have been the home for many of our wild flowers, at least according to the records of Greek physicians. It was Dioscorides who mentioned the Grass of Parnassus growing on the mountain, even though it was the Flemish botanist Mathias de l'Obel who is credited with coining the name for the flower when he was captivated by its beauty and called it *gramen Parnassi*.

The plant has all the appearances of being a honey plant. When the sun shines on it the flowers smell faintly of honey, but the plant does not contain any nectar and its main use in medicine has been for complaints of the liver, leading to the local name of 'White Liverwort'. A decoction of the leaves was thought to settle upset stomachs and could also dispel kidney stones if taken in wine or water.

Perennial	
Size:	3 – 8in (7.5 – 20cm)
Flowers:	July – October
Sowing:	Sow the seeds in March in trays and plant out when large enough to handle. Alternatively, sow direct into open ground in late April. Divide or plant in Spring.
Position:	Ordinary garden soil, but will only thrive in a damp situation.
Note:	Needs space and should not be crowded by stronger plants. Rock gardens and poolsides.

Golden Rod

Solidago virgaurea

Aaron's Rod, Cast-the-Spear, Farewell Summer.

Golden Rod was considered a valuable 'wound' herb, useful in applications to bruises, cuts and particularly, wounds suffered by weapon cuts. For this it was applied either externally to the affected areas or else taken internally as a tonic. Gerard esteemed it 'above all other herbs' for these curative properties, and Culpeper mentions that it had long been considered famous as a 'wound' herb. In fact, it became so popular that during the reign of Elizabeth I supplies ran so low it was imported from the Continent, particularly Germany and possibly also from America. In the American Continent the numerous related kinds of Golden Rod are far more prolific than in England and are considered to be weeds. It is a little surprising, therefore, to find that the English cultivated it as a garden plant. Perhaps they had in mind something of the old beliefs regarding Golden Rod. It was said that Golden Rod could reveal the location of buried treasure and that if the plant grew close to one's house then good fortune, or indeed, riches would be visited upon the household.

The modern cultivated Golden Rod was developed from stock brought into England by the sixteenth century horticulturist John Tradescant. In the wild, the Golden Rod grows anything up to three feet in height with clusters of small yellow flowers. The North American Indians used these flowers to cure beestings.

Perennial	
Size:	12 – 24in (30 – 60cm)
Flowers:	July – September
Sowing:	Sow either in open ground in early Spring or in trays in Autumn to over-winter in protected area. Plant new stock in November. Divide in either Spring or Autumn.
Position:	Prefers sandy soil although will grow on good ordinary soil. Full sun. A spreading plant.

Golden Rod

Mayweed

Matricaria perforata

*Maid Weed, Maidewode, Maithes, Maudlin,
Mazes, Moonwort.*

The attractive and free-flowering
Mayweed, with its large white flowers, is
related to the Chamomile and makes up a
rather confusing family of plants.

The Scentless Mayweed, which has also
been called *Matricaria inodora* and *M.
maritima*, is often confused with the
similar Corn Chamomile and the Scented
Mayweed. The Scented Mayweed,
Matricaria recutita, is slender and rather
more upright in its appearance than the
Scentless Mayweed and has smaller
flowers.

The generic name for the Mayweeds
was taken from the Latin *matrix*, a womb,
and the plants have often been considered
good for female, uterine diseases.
However, the Latin name for the plant has
also been thought to be from the Latin
mata cara meaning 'beloved mother' and
the plant has been referred to St Anne, the
Mother of the Virgin Mary.

Together with the Plantain and Nettle,
the Mayweed was included in the Anglo-
Saxon 'Nine Herbs Charm', an
enumeration of the nine most effective
and magical herbs used to combat all
known forms of poisoning.

The common name Mayweed refers
not to the month of May, as the plant
does not in fact flower until June, but to
the word 'may' from the Old English
maeg and the Danish *mó*, both an archaic
form of the word for a maiden or young
woman.

Harebell

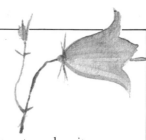

Harebell

Campanula rotundifolia

Bellflower, Bluebell, Ding-Dongs, Lady's Thimbles, Sheep's Bells, Witch Bells, Witches Thimbles.

Mayweed

Despite the fact that the Bluebell *Hyacinthoides non-scripta*, also grows in Scotland, the Harebell is the true Scottish Bluebell. The two are not related. The Bluebell is of the Lily family while Harebell is of the Campanula clan. The confusion has existed for many years, perpetuated by many poets and writers. Shakespeare called the common Bluebell the 'Harebell' in *Cymbeline*, and even Gerard, when speaking of the Bluebell refers to the 'English jacinth or Harebels, thought to grow more plentifully in England than elsewhere'.

While the Bluebell is considered a pretty innocent plant the Harebell has been ascribed certain darker associations. The 'hare' of the common name refers less to the slender stems than to the witch-favourite animal the hare. In Ireland the Gaelic for the Harebell links it with the thimbles belonging to goblins.

The plant should never be picked, as one of the local names suggested that it belonged to the Devil, 'Old Man's Bells'. It is extremely doubtful whether the plant has any medicinal benefits even though the shape of the flowers suggested the throat, and gargles were once popular.

Mayweed	
Annual	
Size:	12 – 24in (20 – 60cm)
Flowers:	June – October
Sowing:	Sow under glass in March, pricking out into boxes and growing-on under glass until planting out in April or May. Alternatively, sow in open ground in April where intended to flower.
Position:	Ordinary garden soil. Border plant.

Harebell	
Perennial	
Size:	6 – 18in (15 – 45cm)
Flowers:	July – September
Sowing:	Sow seeds in cold frame in March. Thin seedlings to 4in (10cm) apart and set out plants in Autumn, 15in (37.5cm) apart. Division can take place in either Autumn or Spring. Ensure good amount of soil taken with roots.
Position:	Border or rockery, open sunny position well-drained soil with some humus.

Bog Asphodel

Narthecium ossifragum

*Limmerick, Maiden's Hair, Moor Grass,
Yellow Grass.*

The Bog Asphodel had an unfortunate reputation among farmers at one time that its mere presence caused cattle and sheep to break their bones. However, it is far more probable that this belief was due more to the actual terrain in which the

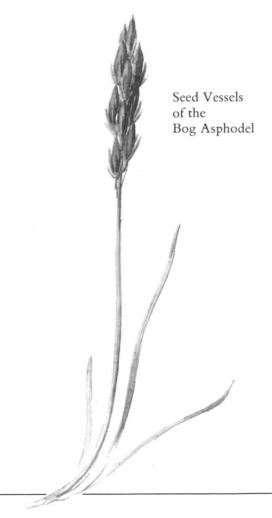

Seed Vessels
of the
Bog Asphodel

Bog Asphodel grew, rather than anything mysterious about the plant. It is largely confined to the boggy and 'tussocky' areas of moorland throughout Britain.

Central flower spikes rise from slender, iris-like, pointed leaves and the brilliant saffron-coloured flowers crown the central stem.

In Shetland this saffron colour prompted people to use the flowers as a readily available substitute for saffron both in medicine and in certain dyeing processes, whilst in Lancashire the Bog Asphodel was collected by local women during the seventeenth century and used by them to impart a 'saffron' colour to their hair.

But surely the strangest 'suggested' medicinal cure for the Bog Asphodel came from the ancient Greeks. The generic name was derived from the Greek word *narthex* meaning 'a hollow stemmed plant' and was used by them to cure the wind. In particular, the type of wind developed from Bacchanalian repasts.

Perennial	
Size:	4 – 15in (10 – 37.5cm)
Flowers:	July – September
Sowing:	Seeds can be sown in a covered frame in March and planted out in Autumn. Or sow direct into open ground in Autumn where intended to flower. Plant in either Autumn or Spring. Divide at same time of year.
Position:	Best in very moist peaty soil in partial shade. Do not allow to dry out in Summer months.

September
to
December

Although what may be termed the 'wild flower season' is now drawing to a close many flowers still adorn the countryside and the Ragwort, Yellow Toadfax and the Clovers may even continue into October, given favourable weather.

September, the Anglo Saxon *gerstmonath*, the month of barley, is also the harvest month, in more ways than one, and while many wild flower seeds can be gathered at other times of the year September is, more or less, the final month for harvesting. This also applies to the fruits of wild shrubs such

119

as the Wild Rose whose hips and 'haws' are now bright red and ripe for picking, and contain more Vitamin C than the fruits of the Blackcurrant. September is also 'conker' month when the fruits of the Horse and the Sweet Chestnut, the Beech, Service and the Hazel combine with a rich store of Blackberries, Elderberries, Sloes and Crab Apples to make this the 'season of mists and mellow fruitfulness' which Keats so loved.

During September and the Autumn months full advantage should be taken of any good, clear weather and the occasional Indian summer to complete the general tasks of clearing the garden and digging over the ground in order to allow Winter frosts to break down the consistency, ready for the following year.

There are also several important tasks which will occupy much of our time. The planting out of seedlings into their required flowering positions – although plants such as the Red Campion and the Alkanet could well suffer if the Winter is particularly hard – the division of established plants and their transferral to new sites, and the sowing of new seed.

Apart from the many flowers whose seed can be sown direct into open ground in the Autumn, now is also the time to sow those that particularly require the action of Winter frosts to break down the hard outer seed husk, by either sowing in open ground or in prepared trays left outdoors to take advantage of the cold weather.

But all the hard work and preparation which is done during the Autumn will be amply rewarded during the following year's wild flower season.

Planning
and
Cultivation

The heralds of Spring – Primroses, *Primula vulgaris*.

Planning the Garden

Any gardener, faced with a seed merchant's catalogue, will ask himself certain basic questions regarding his plot of land. What type of soil do I have and what variety of plants will be suitable for this soil? Is that soil chalk, loam, clay, sand or downright poor? Does the garden have a southern or a northern aspect? Is it exposed to the elements or a secluded suntrap? Many of these questions are very basic and very often subconscious, yet these same questions apply to the growing of wild flowers as they do for the more usual cultivated garden flowers.

Wild flowers are no more difficult to grow than are ordinary flowers. There is no special mystique attached to their cultivation.

Yet there is one thing which can be done which could well ease the task of deciding exactly which flowers to choose. In very much the same way as the aspiring flower and vegetable gardener will check what varieties grow well locally, so too with wild flowers. Consider first what wild flowers exist in your immediate neighbourhood. Particularly if you are fortunate enough to live within easy reach of open countryside, take a walk around the area and see what is growing in the hedgerows and fields. Chances are that the same soil conditions which suit those wild flowers will make up the basic soil of your garden. But remember that if your greatest wish is to grow a wild flower which only thrives in moorland pastures in the north of England, do not be surprised if it is rather more difficult to establish in your shaded, warm, wooded valley in the heart of southern rural England. Choose those plants which are known to have similar habitats to those which you either already possess or which you can duplicate in your garden.

One of the underlying reasons for concentrating on areas of wild flowers in the garden is, surely, a wish to preserve something of those days, regrettably distant, when they were more plentiful. But also, and probably more importantly, there is a desire to halt the possible extinction of some species of wild flower. These scarcer plants require your help. Fortunately these days there are schemes in certain parts of the country for the re-introduction of flowers such as the Primrose onto grass verges and hedgebanks, yet the beautiful Cowslip and Pasque Flower could do with your help in averting the rapid gallop to scarcity and eventual extinction.

Growing from Seed

Personally, I would not encourage the collection of seeds from the wild. There should be as little disturbance of the wild plants in their natural habitats as possible, for fear of breaking down an often delicate natural balance.

But there are two ways in which you can obtain seeds for wild flowers. Either from the established plants in your own garden, or from an established seedsman. Fortunately there are now an ever increasing number of seed merchants who are specialising in wild flowers. These seedsmen grow wild flowers specifically for the seeds and, very often, many varieties which you might find difficult to gather yourself. Then, once plants are established, you can collect seeds from your own plants. This can be great fun – particularly if you have patience and are not too easily discouraged.

With the increasing number of gardeners growing wild flowers there is also a chance that a neighbour is already growing the plant you are after. It is not outside the realms of possibility that this gardener could be encouraged to part with seeds, cuttings and, more importantly, information.

Seed Collection

The larger the seed the easier it is to harvest. Violets, on the other hand, due to the size and position of the plant, the smallness of the seeds and the fact that the Violet drops them very quickly when ripe, can pose a very real problem. But the larger plants and larger seeds are relatively easy. One of the best methods is to tie a bag of muslin around the seed head or seed pods before they are fully ripe (see below). Later, pick off the head and then extract the seeds from inside the muslin bag. Dry off these seeds and store in paper envelopes (in the same way that commercial seeds are stored) keeping them in a dry, well-ventilated place at an even, fairly low temperature, until required.

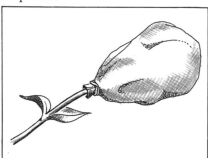 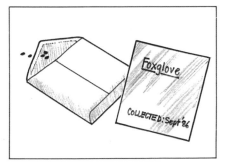

Seed harvesting should be carried out on a dry, sunny day and when the plant is just about to release its seeds in the normal way. When the seed is ripe it either drops from the wild flower or is transported elsewhere by the wind or by attachment to passing animals, eventually to fall to the ground. There it lies awaiting the correct conditions for germination. This time-lapse, between leaving the flower and germination, varies from flower to flower and some of the seeds require a little help if you are not to wait for natural germination to take place – a process that can sometimes take anything up to a couple of seasons to complete.

Certain seeds require the action upon them of winter frosts and extremes of cold in order to break down the hard outer husk of the seed. There are two ways of doing this. One is to place the seeds in a plastic container of sand or peat and put this into a refrigerator for about two months prior to spring sowing. Alternatively, place the seeds, well buried, in the same type of mixture of sand or peat, in a tray *(below, left)*. Place the tray outdoors during the winter months in a position to receive the full effects of the cold weather; a piece of wire netting over it will avoid the attention of birds or other animals. In the spring the young seedlings can be planted out, either in open ground or into a reserve bed, in the normal way. Bluebells and Coltsfoot flowers fall into this 'stratification' category.

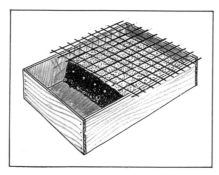
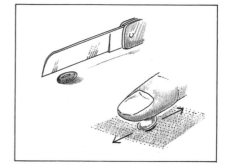

Whilst many of the long-lasting seeds, such as the Poppy, are very small and, in the natural course of events germinate when brought to the surface after the ground has been disturbed, other relatively large leguminous seeds, such as Vetches and Clovers, should be rubbed gently with sandpaper *(above, right)*, or a small incision made in the outer husk before sowing in open ground.

Seed Sowing

Apart from those wild flowers whose seeds can be sown direct into open ground in your garden there are many which you may wish to sow in trays and pots up to seedling stage, and then plant out in their flowering positions. For this a good standard seed compost such as John Innes is very suitable for most varieties. This compost is made up of sterilised medium loam, fibrous peat and coarse sand with superphosphate of lime and ground chalk also being added.

Division

Plants which become overcrowded in an area and those that would benefit from moving to a newer area to increase their number can be divided up. Those plants having many fibrous roots are relatively easy to divide.

After flowering, dig up the whole clump, shake off any loose soil and simply pull apart by hand. Select or pull away the sections of root which do not show signs of being too woody or which have obviously died off and then replant in the required position. If the root system is any larger, then using two garden forks back to back and pushing in opposite directions will divide up the system successfully *(below, left)*. With plants which make runners, young plantlets at the ends of these can be detached and planted elsewhere *(below, right)*, as long as they have begun to make their own roots.

Certain plants such as the Daffodil and the Bluebell produce small bulbs in addition to the main one. These are called offshoots, and if detached carefully from the main bulb these can be planted elsewhere. If they appear rather inferior, but still warrant the effort, pot them on in a suitable potting compost; but they may take a few years before flowering.

Garden Plans

In the same way that no garden soil referred to in the gardening manuals will ever match, exactly, the soil present in your own particular garden area, so too can no suggested plans for a garden ever hope to solve all of the problems posed by your own patch of ground. At the very best, parts of the suggested plans will correspond with certain areas which you are considering.

The first step is to find out what you have in the garden at the moment. Draw up as accurate a plan of the garden as possible, noting down all exterior dimensions, and then draw this up on graph paper. Then record positions of all existing shrubs and vegetation and the nature of the soil, whether it is damp or extremely dry, composed of clay or sandy and whether it varies throughout its length. Note also areas of shade and those sections exposed to the elements, and which parts face north or south. Note down as much as is relevant, yet there is no need to be so excessively detailed that each blade of grass is recorded! This plan will be used as reference when constructing a second plan, which will include the intended positions of new planting.

If you already have an established garden with areas devoted to certain favourite plants do not flatten everything with the intention of converting the whole garden to the growing of wild flowers. Introduce them gradually, replanning and replanting area by area. The gradual approach to introducing wild varieties is much less trouble than the wholesale redesign of a garden.

Before deciding which plants you wish to cultivate there are certain points to bear in mind. Many wild flowers are not the farmer's favourite. Depending upon your location, and the proximity of arable land, consider very carefully whether you can control the growth and natural reproduction of certain plants. If in doubt consult your local farming organisations and the farmer whose field borders your property. If grown in fairly small numbers there is less reason for concern, but check first.

PLAN 1

Plan 1 takes a conventional shape and one which will be familiar to many urban gardeners – fairly flat, rigidly rectangular with standard fencing on all three sides away from the house, and with a small garden shed in the north-western corner. The soil is assumed to be neutral or slightly limy.

The first requirement is to break down the rigid feel to the garden layout by altering the shape of the 'side lines'. Instead of the narrow, strip borders running down both sides, curved borders have been created to form two irregular 'herbaceous' style borders with plants of varying height.

Along the northern side of the garden the plants nearest to the house are fairly low-lying, but with the overall height of the plants increasing as they near the shed. On the southern side, highly scented wild flowers predominate close to the house and, where the border narrows, and a certain amount of shade covers the ground, Violets and Ground Ivy can be grown.

The very bottom of the garden will get some shade from the Honeysuckle and the whole of this area has been devoted to those plants which will attract butterflies and insects, such as Thistles and Nettles. Poppies occupy the poorer ground close to the shed.

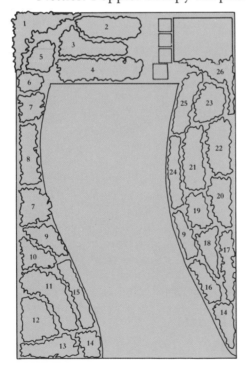

1	Honeysuckle	16	Milkwort
2	Nettles	17	Tufted Vetch
3	Thistles	18	Wild Madder
4	Poppy	19	Red Campion
5	Ragged Robin	20	Rosebay Willow Herb
6	Snowdrop		
7	Ground Ivy	21	Oxeye Daisy
8	Dog Violet	22	Yellow Flag
9	Sweet Violet	23	Sneezewort
10	Purple Loosestrife	24	Buttercup
		25	Toadflax
11	Ladies Bedstraw	26	Dog Rose
12	Meadowsweet		
13	Mayweed		
14	Heartsease		
15	Daisy		

Average Soil

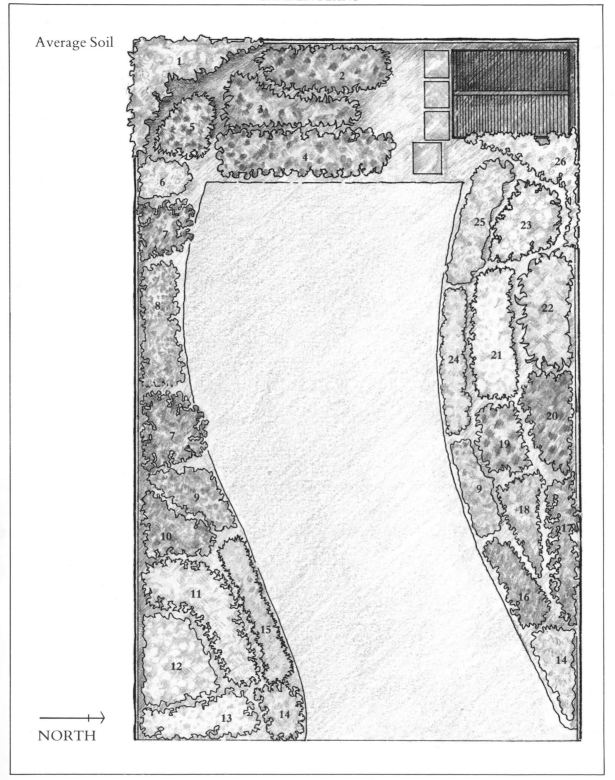

NORTH

PLAN 2

With *Plan 2* we have taken the same garden, with the same overall dimensions but with soil which is more acid. This does not mean that a complete change of flowers should take place, as many of the flowers considered will take to most soils, but the acidity favours the tall, spiky Agrimony and the common, but no less beautiful, Bluebell. Both plants can be introduced along with shorter plants such as Marsh Marigold and the Dusky Cranesbill.

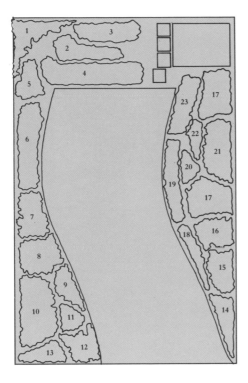

1 Honeysuckle
2 Thistle
3 Nettle
4 Heather
5 Wood Sorrel
6 Cowslip
7 Forget-me-Not
8 Bluebell
9 Primrose
10 St John's Wort
11 Marsh Marigold
12 Tormentil
13 Herb Robert
14 Coltsfoot
15 Devil's Bit Scabious
16 Agrimony
17 Bellflower
18 Creeping Cinquefoil
19 Buttercup
20 Dusky Cranesbill
21 Foxglove
22 Spearwort
23 Marsh Violet

Acid-based
Soil

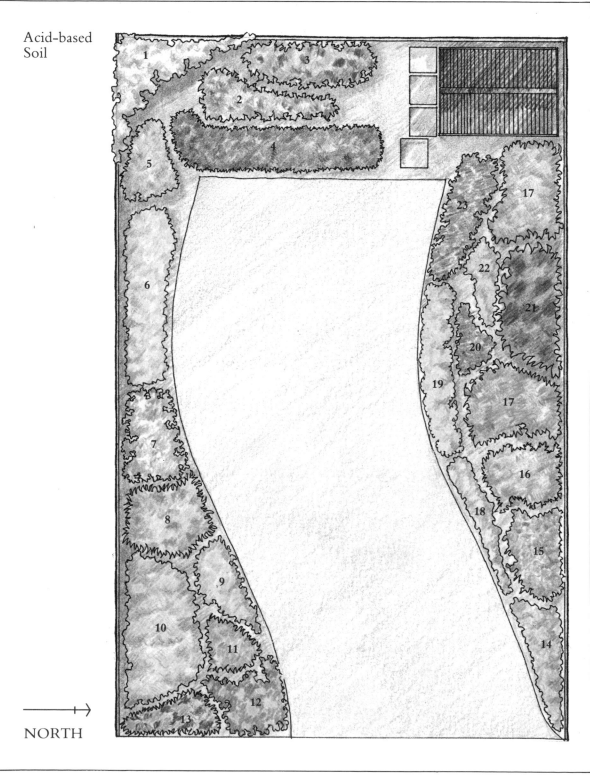

NORTH

PLAN 3

Plan 3 is again based upon the same basic layout but with a very much damper soil. A pool has been introduced into the south-western corner and a rockery next to the house on the southern side. The tallest, damp-loving plants have generally been grouped behind the pool area in order to frame it. Behind both the rockery area and the northern bed the climbing Honeysuckle and Meadow Vetch have been planted in order to break up the rigid fencing on either side of the garden.

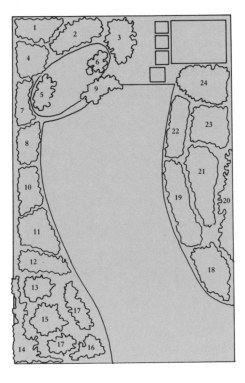

1   Great Hairy
    Willow Herb
2   Yellow
    Loosestrife
3   Ladies Smock
4   Yellow Flag
5   White Water
    Lily
6   Yellow Water
    Lily
7   Foxglove
8   Marsh Marigold
9   Water Forget-
    me-Not
10 Purple Orchis
11 Wood Anemone
12 Periwinkle
13 Bugle
14 Meadow Vetch
15 Ladies Smock
16 Saxifrage
17 Cinquefoil
18 Ragwort
19 Primrose
20 Honeysuckle
21 Daffodil
22 Lesser Celandine
23 Bellflower
24 Ramson

Damp Soil

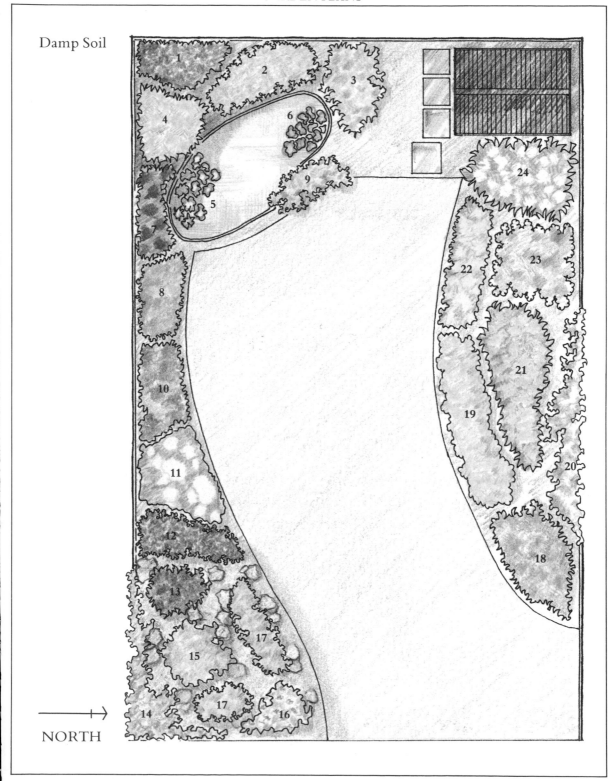

NORTH

PLAN 4

Plan 4 features a traditional Elizabethan-style knot garden. These popular gardens probably originated in Italy and came to England via Holland with many of the intricate designs being very reminiscent of the decorative architectural style prevalent in Holland at that time.

Generally the knot garden was rectangular, with hedges of dwarf Box or Rosemary, and infilled with low-growing plants and even coloured gravels.

The arrangement featured here relies upon a low hedge of Box or Lavender to about 12 inches high, with the areas for flowers designed for yellow and white flowers in the outermost sections, and then blue and violet colours towards the centre. This arrangement of hedges is very simple in design, though some original 'knots' were, as the name suggests, very much more intricate.

1 Buttercup
2 *Wood Anemone
3 Daisy
4 Primrose
5 Periwinkle
6 Heartsease
7 Sweet Violet
8 Dog Violet
9 Foxglove

Hedges of Box or
Lavender

Knot Garden

Average Soil

PLAN 5

Plan 5 deals with a very much smaller garden area. This could be either an island site, the last unpaved area of a courtyard, or even an area which you deliberately devote to wild flowers as an experiment.

Being of a much more manageable size you can give your ideas full rein, particularly as the soil is also easy to adapt to your particular requirements. This plan features a massed display of flowers to give a feeling of lushness and profusion with some of the plants specifically chosen to overhang or overrun the edge of the area. The general arrangement is for the highest point to be off-centre and the rest of the plants reducing in height gradually, down to the four sides and corners.

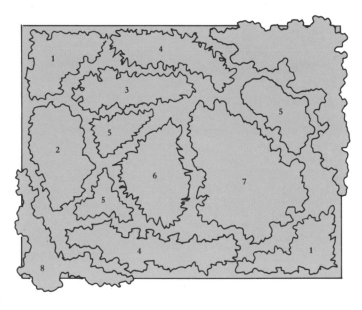

1   Eyebright
2   Primrose
3   Lesser Celandine
4   Common Avens
5   Speedwell
6   Mayweed
7   Nettle-Leaved
      Bellflower
8   Wild Strawberry

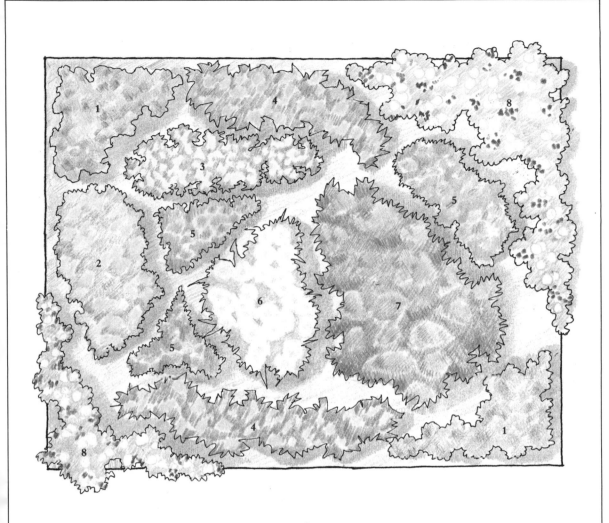

Rich Humus

PLAN 6

The final plan, *Plan 6*, is included to show what effects can be created with the varieties of wild flower which are classed as climbers. Where there are areas which you wish screened from the house, either for privacy or because not everyone wishes to see a compost heap all the time, these climbing varieties come into their own. Also a number of years have elapsed and the bottom section of our 'standard' garden has developed a hedge with young oaks, another area for encouraging both those plants which climb and those which require a certain amount of dappled shade. This banked area is also ideal for the mixing of grasses and suitable wild flowers.

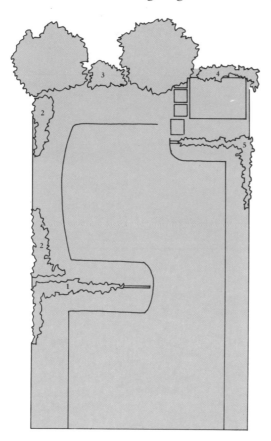

1 Dog Rose
2 Honeysuckle
3 Tufted Vetch
4 Bindweed
5 Bittersweet

Within shaded area:
Wood Sorrel
Celandine
Wood Anemone
Wood Crowfoot
Herb Robert
Cowslip

Average Soil

NORTH

Wildlife in the Garden

A flat-bodied Dragonfly hovering on Rosemary.

Birds, butterflies and other insects

Birds feature very prominently in any garden situation, particularly in a garden containing a variety of wild flowers, as they search for their food from fruits, seeds and insects. During Spring, and particularly Autumn, when migrating birds use the garden as a resting place during their travels, they greatly appreciate the inclusion in the garden of such plants as the Nettle and Thistle – and, in fact, any plants which have been left to go to seed. Both the Nettles and Thistles harbour rich varieties of insect life such as the caterpillars of the Peacock and Red Admiral butterflies and also certain grubs which might otherwise become pests for the gardener. Even the lowly Forget-me-Nots and Daisies are very important to Tits and Finches, and during the Winter months the fruits of the Blackberry, Hawthorn, Honeysuckle and other fruit-bearing shrubs supply much needed nourishment for Blackbirds, Thrushes and other birds.

There are two very good reasons for encouraging butterflies and other such insects into the 'wild flower' garden. Firstly there is the obvious, inestimable pleasure to be gained from the sight of these beautiful creatures as they flit from flower to flower about the garden – a reminder of the times when both they and the flowers which you are trying to encourage were far more common.

Yet the main source of pleasure surely comes from the realisation that you are, in some small way at least, helping to restore something of the original, natural balance which existed between flowers and wildlife. The lives of both wild flowers and insects are inter-related, each depending upon the other for their very existence, and by cultivating certain flowers you will be supplying valuable sources of nectar for bees and butterflies and they, in their turn, ensuring the pollination of your wild flowers.

Pollination, in botanical terms, means the actual transference of the dusty, fertilising pollen produced by the stamen of one flower to the stigma of another. Fertilisation of the ovary of the flower then takes place and the essential seeds are developed.

There are two ways in which this process can take place, either by self-pollination or by cross-pollination.

In self-pollination, the pollen from the stamen can be transferred to the stigma of the same flower, or other flowers on the same plant, at just the right time when both are ripe.

Cross-pollination has to take place when the plants are uni-sexual. These do not possess both stamens and stigma together on one plant and must, somehow, exchange pollen to another plant, sometimes over quite a distance. This is most frequently done by insects. In order for this to take place the flowers must attract the 'carriers' in some way, either visually or by scent. Bees, in fact, visit a far greater number of flowers than do any other insects. Their object is the collection of the sweet, juicy nectar secreted by those flowers. This they collect and return to the hive. After a few days this nectar is converted into honey and provides the bees with a valuable future food store.

In the process of collection, pollen from the flower becomes dusted onto the back of the bee and when that bee later visits another plant the pollen is transferred to the stigma and fertilisation can take place.

In some cases flowers have special devices to prevent self-pollination where they carry both stamens and stigma.

Perhaps the most interesting illustration of this resultant cross-pollination process occurs with the Primrose. The flowers are made up of five petals at the end of a flower tube and they can be of two differing designs. Some have anthers at the top of the flower tube with the stigma below them and about half-way down the tube. These are called 'thrum-eyed' primroses. The opposite arrangement, called 'pin-eyed', have the anthers below the stigma. In both varieties the nectar is still contained at the base of the flower tube. Consequently, when a bee visits the Primrose and heads for the nectar, pollen from the stigma of a 'thrum-eyed' Primrose is

deposited in the correct position on the bee's body so that, when – and only when – that bee visits a 'pin-eyed' Primrose the pollen will be transferred to the anthers.

The methods by which flowers attract bee visitors are quite complex. Bees are colour-blind in the red area of the spectrum and cannot distinguish between red and green. This explains why many of the regular bee plants have yellow or blue flowers. However, the bees do not necessarily see the same colour as we do, because they have high sensitivity to ultra-violet light; to them a yellow flower is effectively purple. Flowers often carry guide-lines, as in wild Pansies, or central marks like the yellow zone round the throat of the Forget-me-not, which help insects to find the nectar point. In many flowers these markings are invisible to the human eye but are picked up by the ultra-violet-sensitive bee eye. Some flowers also have ridges leading towards the nectar area.

It is not scent which primarily attracts bees but the colour and design of flowers. Experiments have been conducted which prove this. A blue-petalled flower, which had been visited by bees, had its petals removed overnight. The following day the bees no longer visited the flower, although nectar still remained in the flower tube.

Butterflies, *Lepidoptera*, on the other hand, are attracted more often by the scent of a flower rather more than by its looks. In many cases the butterfly will visit those flowers with a similar scent to that of the butterfly itself. It was probably this scent of butterflies which led to them being referred to as the 'Flowers of the Air'. Colour and also the shape of flowers are often important to many butterflies.

Yet butterflies are only temporary visitors to the garden. Many have a relatively short flying season and their only object in visiting your garden is to feed upon the plants which you have so graciously provided for them. Then they will depart, but perhaps leaving their eggs behind. So to attract these beautiful visitors to the garden it would be wise to cultivate the very flowers which they specially like. The following details regarding the more common butterflies, together with the list on page 149 of the flowers mentioned in this book and which are objects of butterfly attention, may help you to decide which plants to encourage.

Brimstone (*Gonepteryx rhamni***)**
Bright lemon yellow with an orange spot in the centre of each wing.
The female is similarly marked, but greenish yellow. 2¼in (5.25cm).
The caterpillars feed upon Buckthorn and Alder. The butterflies visit
many flowers for the nectar, including Thistles and Knapweed. Two
broods March – June and July – September.

Clouded Yellow (*Colias croceus***)**
A migrant from Southern Europe and common in South Eastern
England in season. 2in (5cm). Male is rich yellow-orange with dark
outlines while the female has same background but with more
pronounced brown markings. Caterpillars feed on Clover, Bird's
Foot Trefoil and other leguminous plants. May – October.

Comma (*Polygonia c-album***)**
Both sexes very similar. Reddish brown with dark markings the
edges of the wings of a very ragged design with numerous 'curls'.
Caterpillars feed on Stinging Nettles and the butterflies are very
frequent visitors to the garden. 1¾in (4.5cm) March – October.

Common Blue (*Polyommatus icarus***)**
The commonest blue butterfly in Britain. Found almost anywhere in
the countryside. 1¼in (3cm). Male is clear bluish-violet with white
and black margins. Female dull brown with sprinkling of white dots
and orange patches at outer edge of wings. Caterpillars feed on
Bird's Foot Trefoil, Clover and butterfly upon Fleabane and
Marjoram. Active during sunny days. June – September.

Dingy Skipper (*Erynnis tages***)**
Small butterfly, 1in (2.5cm) wingspan, pale brown with circular dots
on fore-wings. Female similar. Caterpillars feed on Bird's Foot
Trefoil. April – June.

Dark Green Fritillary (*Argynnis aglaja***)**
The top side of this fritillary is a rich brown with numerous dark
brown markings, the underside having a greenish hue. 2½in
(6.5cm). The female is duller in colouring. Caterpillar food is the
Violet and the butterfly feeds on tall Thistles. July – August.

Duke–of–Burgundy Fritillary (*Hamearis lucina***)**
Smaller than the Dark Brown Fritillary, 1in (2.5cm), but with
similar markings. Female also similar. Often frequents woodland
rides and clearings. Caterpillars feed on the Primrose and the
Cowslip. May – August.

Gatekeeper (*Pyronia tithonus***)**
Also called the Hedge Brown. Small, golden-brown butterfly with dark brown markings, widespread in the West of England and the South. As name implies it frequents hedgerows feeding on Bramble blossom. Eggs laid on grasses. August – September.

Green Hairstreak (*Callophrys rubi***)**
The commonest and most widely spread Hairstreak and noted for unusual aerobatics. Both male and female very similar, but male has small dot on fore-edge of wing. 1in (2.5cm). Common in hedgerows and visits gardens in search of Broom and Bird's Foot Trefoil. Caterpillars feed on Gorse and Bramble. May – June.

Grizzled Skipper (*Pyrgus malvae***)**
Very small wing span, under 1in (2.5cm) this butterfly indulges in rapid flight close to the ground. Male and female similar with almost black wings with grey markings. Common in Southern Britain. Caterpillars feed on low growing plants such as Strawberry, Cinquefoils and Brambles. Late March – June and second brood in July – September.

Marbled White (*Melanargia galathea***)**
1½in (3.75cm). White and cream ground with darker brown markings predominating. Female larger with fewer dark markings. Caterpillars feed on Colt's Foot and wild grasses. Butterfly visits Thistles and Scabious. Slow flight. Limestone and chalk areas in South of England. Mid-July to August.

Meadow Brown (*Maniola jurtina***)**
Common grey-brown butterfly with black spot on centre of each fore-wing. 1¾in (4.5cm). Slow flight. Caterpillars feed on grasses and butterfly on Thistles and meadow flowers. Late June – September.

Orange Tip (*Anthocharis cardamines***)**
Male has white colouring with front of fore-wings orange with black outline. Female has no orange colouring. Well distributed throughout Britain, less so in Scotland and Ireland. Caterpillars feed on Hedge Mustard and Cuckoo Flower and other cruciferous plants. April and May.

Painted Lady (*Vanessa cardui***)**
Very common in gardens. 2¼ (6cm). Light reddish-brown ground with darker markings on front of fore-wings and lighter markings

elsewhere. Rapid powerful flight. Elaborate courtship display lasting several days. Butterfly feeds on Thistles, Mallows and Stinging Nettles. Eggs laid on Stinging Nettles. June – August.

Peacock (*Inachis io*)

Common in gardens and parks throughout Britain. 2¼in (6cm). Both sexes have noticeable red wings with black markings on fore-wings containing 'eyes' in pale blue and cream. Caterpillars raised on Stinging Nettles while butterfly frequents Agrimony and Buddleia. Often enters houses in winter. April – August.

Red Admiral (*Vanessa atalanta*)

Familiar visitor to gardens and parks. Widespread. 2½in (6.25cm). Strong flight, roosting in trees at night. Visits many wild flowers and fond of over-ripe fruit. Caterpillars feed on Stinging Nettles. June – August.

Silver-washed Fritillary (*Argynnis paphia*)

Woodland butterfly and common in South and West of England. 2½in (6.25cm). Male bright orange with dark brown blobs towards outer edge of wings. Female lighter in colour. Butterflies frequent Brambles in large numbers. Caterpillar feeds on Dog Violets. Mid-July.

Small Garden White (*Pieris rapea*)

1¾in (4.5cm). Male white with black dot in centre of front wings and black edging. Female pale, buff-coloured with dark tips to wings two black dots on fore-wings and single dot on back wings. Very common. Like the Large White it likes Cabbages and Brussels Sprouts, where it lays its eggs. April – August.

Small Tortoiseshell (*Aglais urticae*)

The commonest British butterfly. Golden-brown colour with violet-blue markings along all wing edges. Female similar. Gardens and parks throughout Britain. Small Tortoiseshells chase each other around the garden in erratic flight. Caterpillar feeds on Stinging Nettle and butterfly feeds on a variety of wild flowers, Buddleia and Michaelmas Daisy. 2in (5cm). June – October.

Speckled Wood (*Pararge aegeria*)

1¾in (4cm). Black and brown colouring marked with a few cream blotches on fore-wings and three black and white dots on back wing. Female lighter in colouring and larger. Feeds on garden flowers but prefers shade and dappled sunlight. Caterpillars feed on Coltsfoot and grasses. Two broods from April to October.

Wall Brown (Lassiommata megera)
1¾in (4cm). Common in Britain. Uncultivated ground and country lanes. Caterpillars feed on common grasses while butterfly is attracted to wild flowers and will bask on walls, pathways and stony banks. Male has brown colouring with darker markings overlaid and a black dot with white centre on fore-wings. Female lighter and larger. Two broods April to September.

Moths

Moths also play an important part in the process of pollination. There are more moths than there are butterflies in Britain, yet only a few of the more common varieties fit into the scheme of things in the wild flower garden. Most moths confine their flying activities to the night-time, except for the Cinnabar and the Burnet moths which fly during the daytime. The distinctly coloured Cinnabar, with its dramatic red and black colouring, may well fly during daylight hours as it has so few predators. It is poisonous to birds who, having once tried it, are unlikely to try again.

The flowers which moths feed on tend to be of delicate appearance and either pale yellow or white. Many of these flowers only open at night, remaining closed for the daylight hours, effectively guarding the nectar within and ensuring that when they open the full effect of their scent is produced.

Of the more common moths the large Elephant Hawk moth feeds on the Rosebay Willow Herb and the Bedstraws at night, and the rest of the Hawk moth family on Honeysuckle and Convolvulus flowers. Caterpillars of both the Emperor and Oak Eggar moths feed on Brambles, Heather and Broom and the Garden Tiger moth on Nettles and Dandelions. Many of the moths, in fact, feed on the very flowers which are so attractive to butterflies, be they the taller plants such as Rosebay Willow Herb or shorter, ground-hugging varieties like the Violet which attract the White Ermine and Wood Tiger moths.

Wild Flowers which will attract Butterflies

Flower	Butterfly	Caterpillar
Agrimony	Peacock	
Bird's Foot Trefoil	Green Hairstreak	Chalkhill Blue Clouded Yellow Common Blue Dingy Skipper Silver-Spotted Skipper Silver-Studded Blue
Bramble	Gatekeeper High Brown Fritillary Silver-Studded Blue Silver-Washed Fritillary White Admiral	Green Hairstreak Grizzled Skipper
Broom	Green Hairstreak	
Bugle	Pearl-Bordered Fritillary	
Cinquefoil		Grizzled Skipper
Clover		Clouded Yellow
Coltsfoot		Marbled White Speckled Wood
Cowslip		Duke-of-Burgundy Fritillary
Devil's Bit Scabious	Marsh Fritillary Marbled White	Marsh Fritillary
Foxglove		Heath Fritillary
Gorse		Green Hairstreak Silver-Studded Blue
Ground Ivy		Checkered Skipper
Heather	Large Heath Silver-Studded Blue	Silver-Studded Blue
Honeysuckle		Marsh Fritillary White Admiral
Ladies Smock	Orange Tip	

Flower	Butterfly	Caterpillar
Nettles		Comma
		Small Tortoiseshell
		Peacock
		Red Admiral
Parsley		Swallowtail
Plantain		Heath Fritillary
		Marsh Fritillary
Primrose		Duke-of-Burgundy Fritillary
		Pearl-Bordered Fritillary
Strawberry		Grizzled Skipper
Thistles	Brimstone	Painted Lady
	Dark-Green Fritillary	
	Heath-Brown Fritillary	
	Marbled White	
	Meadow Brown	
	Painted Lady	
	Small Heath	
Tormentil	Large Heath	
Vetch		Adonis Blue
		Chalkhill Blue
		Small Blue

Wild Flower Seeds for Cultivation

Over the past few years the variety of wild flower seeds available from seed merchants has increased remarkably. The following list gives just a representative selection of the many seeds suitable for wild flower garden cultivation. These, together with those plants already mentioned in this book, and the further varieties covered in seed merchants catalogues, now mean that there are well over 1,000 different varieties of wild flower available.

Aconite, Winter
Angelica, Wild
Archangel, Yellow
Avens, Water
Balsam, Indian
Basil-Thyme
Basil, Wild
Bedstraw, Hedge
Bryony, Black
Bur-Marigold, Trifid
Burdock
Burnet-Saxifrage
Calamint
Campion, Bladder
Carrot, Wild
Catchfly
Cat's-Ear
Centaury, Common
Charlock
Chicory
Clary, Meadow
Corncockle
Cornflower
Cranesbill, Bloody
Dandelion
Dropwort
Elecampane

Evening Primrose
Everlasting Pea
Feverfew
Flax, Blue
Fleabane
Gentian, Spring
Goat's-Rue
Gromwell, Common
Ground-Elder
Hawkbit
Hemp-Agrimony
Hop, Wild
Horehound
Hound's-Tongue
Knapweed
Larkspur
Mallow
Marigold, Corn
Medick, Black
Melilot
Michaelmas-Daisy
Mignonette, Wild
Mint, Water
Monk's-Hood
Motherwort
Mullein
Musk Mallow
Oxlip
Pimpernel, Scarlet

Ploughman's-Spikenard
Poppy, Welsh
Restharrow
Rocket, Yellow
Sage, Wood
Sainfoin
Sanicle
Scabious, Field
Selfheal
Sheep's-Bit
Snapdragon
Sow-Thistle
Star-of-Bethlehem
Tansy
Tare, Smooth
Teasel
Thistle, Carline
Thrift
Thyme, Wild
Traveller's-Joy
Valerian
Viper's Bugloss
Wallflower, Wild
Weld
Woodruff, Sweet
Wormwood, Wild
Woundwort, Hedge
Yellow-Rattle

Conservation of Wild Plants and Animals Act

Throughout this book the emphasis has been laid upon the cultivation of wild flowers either from seed or by means of cuttings, often obtained from other like-minded gardeners. One of the prime considerations behind this has been the need for the protection of many endangered plants and the continued preservation of declining species.

There are, in fact, so many seeds available commercially that there should be very little need for any wholesale brigandry of wild plants from their natural habitats. Fortunately we are becoming more aware of our 'responsibilities' regarding our inherited flora; a feeling helped considerably by the Conservation of Wild Plants and Animals Act of 1975. Although the whole Act concerns nature lovers, the sections relating to wild flowers are covered below.

13. Protection of wild plants

(1) Subject to the provisions of this Part, if any person—
    (a) intentionally picks, uproots or destroys any wild plant included in Schedule 8;
    or
    (b) not being an authorised person, intentionally uproots any wild plant not included in that Schedule,
    he shall be guilty of an offence.

(2) Subject to the provisions of this Part, if any person—
    (a) sells, offers or exposes for sale, or has in his possession or transports for the purpose of sale, any live or dead wild plant included in Schedule 8, or any part of, or anything derived from, such a plant;
    or
    (b) publishes or causes to be published any advertisement likely to be understood as conveying that he buys or sells, or intends to buy or sell, any of those things,
he shall be guilty of an offence.

(3) Notwithstanding anything in subsection (1), a person shall not be guilty of an offence by reason of any act made unlawful by that subsection if he shows that the act was an incidental result of a lawful operation and could not reasonably have been avoided.

(4) In any proceedings for an offence under subsection (2)(a), the plant in question shall be presumed to have been a wild plant unless the contrary is shown.

SCHEDULE 8

PLANTS WHICH ARE PROTECTED

Common name

Alison, Small

Broomrape, Bedstraw
Broomrape, Oxtongue
Broomrape, Thistle

Calamint, Wood
Catchfly, Alpine
Cinquefoil, Rock
Club-rush, Triangular
Cotoneaster, Wild
Cow-wheat, Field
Cudweed, Jersey

Diapensia

Eryngo, Field

Fern, Dickie's Bladder
Fern, Killarney

Galingale, Brown
Gentian, Alpine
Gentian, Spring
Germander, Water
Gladiolus, Wild

Hare's-ear, Sickle-leaved
Hare's-ear, Small
Heath, Blue
Helleborine, Red

Knawel, Perennial
Knotgrass, Sea

Lady's-slipper
Lavender, Sea
Leek, Round-headed
Lettuce, Least
Lily, Snowdon

Marsh-mallow, Rough

Orchid, Early Spider
Orchid, Fen
Orchid, Ghost
Orchid, Late Spider
Orchid, Lizard
Orchid, Military
Orchid, Monkey

Pear, Plymouth
Pink, Cheddar
Pink, Childling

Sandwort, Norwegian
Sandwort, Teesdale
Saxifrage, Drooping
Saxifrage, Tufted
Solomon's-seal, Whorled
Sow-thistle, Alpine
Spearwort, Adder's-tongue
Speedwell, Spiked
Spurge, Purple
Starfruit

Violet, Fen

Water-plantain, Ribbon
  leaved
Wood-sedge, Starved
Woodsia, Alpine
Woodsia, Oblong
Wormwood, Field
Woundwort, Downy
Woundwort, Limestone

Yellow-rattle, Greater

Seed Merchants

The following seed merchants specialise in wild flowers and can supply catalogues of their range on request. But please enclose something to cover return postage.

John Chambers
15 Westleigh Road, Barton Seagrave, Kettering, Northants

Chiltern Seeds
Bortree Stile, Ulverston, Cumbria

Mr Fothergill's Seeds
Gazeley Road, Kentford, Newmarket, Suffolk

Naturescape
Little Orchard, Whalton in the Vale, Notts

The Seed Bank
44 Albion Road, Sutton, Surrey

Suffolk Herbs
Sawyers Farm, Little Cornard, Sudbery, Suffolk.

In addition there are certain firms who supply seeds for more general garden flowers and vegetables but which also cover wild flowers.

Samuel Dobie & Son
Llangollen, Clwyd

Suttons Seeds
Torquay, Devon

Thompson & Morgan
Ipswich, Suffolk

Useful Addresses

Many organisations exist whose interests centre around the preservation and cultivation of wild plants and the protection of wildlife. Listed below are a few of the societies whose work relates to the subject of this book.

The British Butterfly Conservation Society
Tudor House, Quorn, Loughborough, Leicestershire.

Council for the Protection of Rural England – C.P.R.E.
4 Hobart Place, London SW1.

Good Gardeners' Association
Arkley Manor Farm, Arkley, Nr Barnet, Hertfordshire.

Hardy Plant Society
10 St Barnabas Road, Emmer Green, Reading, Berkshire.

Herb Society
34 Boscobel Place, London SW1.

Fauna and Flora Preservation Society
Zoological Gardens, Regent's Park, London NW1.

National Council for the Conservation of Plants and Gardens
c/o RHS, Wisley, Woking, Surrey.

Nature Conservancy Council
Northminster House, Peterborough, Northants.

Tradescant Trust
St. Mary's Church, Lambeth, London SE1.

Ulster Trust for Nature Conservation
Barnett's Cottage, Barnett Demesne, Malone Road, Belfast, N. Ireland

Wild Flower Society
69 Outwoods Road, Loughborough, Leics.

In addition, various counties also have their own Trusts for Nature Conservation whose addresses may be found in the area telephone directories.

Bibliography

Banks, Roger, *Old Cottage Garden Flowers* (World's Work, 1983)

Beckett, Kenneth. A, *Growing Hardy Perennials* (Croom Helm, 1981)

Bentham, G., *Handbook of British Flora* (L. Reeve & Co., 1924)

Berrisford, Judith, *The Wild Garden* (Faber, 1966)

Booth, Charles, *An Encyclopedia of Annual and Biennial Garden Plants* (Faber & Faber, 1957)

Brimble, L.F.J., *The Floral Year* (Macmillan, 1949)

Butcher, R.W.A., *A New Illustrated British Flora* (Leonard Hill, 1961)

Chittenden, Fred, *RHS Dictionary of Gardening* (Clarendon Press 1951)

Coats, Alice. M., *The Treasury of Flowers* (Phaidon, 1975)

Coats, Alice. M., *Flowers and Their Histories* (Hulton Press, 1956)

Coley, Hilda. *Wild Flower Preservation* (London, 1933)

Coon, Nelson, *Using Wild and Wayside Plants* (Dover, NY, 1959)

Culpeper, Nicholas, *Complete Herbal* (Manchester, 1826)

De Bray, Lys, *The Wild Garden* (Weidenfeld & Nicholson, 1978)

Dealler, Stephen, *Wild Flowers for the Garden* (Batsford, 1977)

Dony, Perring, Rob, *English Names of Wild Flowers* (Botanical Society , 1974)

Genders, Roy, *The Cottage Garden* (Pelham, 1969)

Genders, Roy, *Hardy Perennials from Seed* (Pelham, 1970)

Gordon, Lesley, *Poorman's Nosegay* (Collins, 1973)

Gordon, Lesley, *A Country Herbal* (Webb & Bower, 1980)

Gordon, Lesley, *Green Magic* (Webb & Bower, 1977)

Grigson, Geoffrey, *The Englishman's Flora* (Phoenix House, 1955)

Hamilton, Edward, *Flora Homeopathica* (London, 1852)

Hatfield, Audrey Wynne, *Pleasure of Wild Plants* (Museum Press, 1966)

Hay, R and Synge, P., *Dictionary of Garden Plants in Colour* (Ebury Press, Michael Joseph, 1969)

Hunt, Doris, *The Flowers of Shakespeare* (Webb & Bower, 1980)

Johnson, George. W., *Gardeners' Dictionary* (George Bell, London, 1875)

Jordan, Michael, *A Guide to Wild Plants* (Millington, 1976)

Launert, Edmund. *Countryside Guide to Edible & Medicinal Plants of Britain and N. Europe* (Hamlyn Group, 1981)

Lovelock, Yann, *The Vegetable Book* (George Allan & Unwin, 1972)

Mabey, Richard. *Food for Free* (Collins, 1972)

McClintock, David, *Companion to Flowers* (Bell, 1966)

Morley, Brian. D., *Wildflowers of the World* (Michael Joseph, 1970)

Morse, Richard, *Introduction to Wild Flowers* (A & C Black, 1949)

Palaiseul, Jean, *Grandmother's Secrets* (Barrie & Jenkins, 1973)

Puttock, A.G., *The Woodland Garden* (Foyle, 1960)

Reader's Digest *Field Guide to the Wild Flowers of Britain* (1981)

Rendell, Vernon, *Wild Flowers in Literature* (1934)

Robinson, William, *The Wild Garden* (The Scolar Press, 1977)

Skinner, Charles. M., *Myths and Legends of Flowers*, (Lippincoat Co., 1911)

Stebbing, M.E., *Colour in the Garden* (Nelson, 1947)

Tyas, Robert, *Language of Flowers* (Routledge & Sons, 1875)

Wilkinson, Lady Caroline. *Weeds and Wild Flowers* (London, 1858)

COUNTRY DIARY Titles published by Webb & Bower,
in association with Michael Joseph

The Country Diary of an Edwardian Lady. *Edith Holden* (1977)

The Edwardian Lady. *The Story of Edith Holden, compiled by Ina Taylor* (1980)

The Country Diary Year Book (1983)

The Country Diary Nature Notes.*Edith Holden/Alan Jenkins* (1984)

The Country Diary Garden Notes. *Edith Holden/Richard Gorer* (1984)

The Country Diary Cookery Notes. *Edith Holden/Alison Harding* (1984)

The Country Diary Companion. *Josephine Poole* (1984)

The Country Diary Book of Crafts. *Annette Mitchell* (1985)

The Country Diary Address Book.(1987)

The Country Diary Birthday Book.(1987)

The Country Diary Book of Knitting. *Annette Mitchell* (1987)

Acknowledgements

The author and publishers would like to thank the many organisations and people who gave advice and information on the production of this book. In particular, the author would especially like to thank Anthony Huxley for his invaluable guidance and help. John Glover for his photographs on pages 6, 15, 121, 126, 127, 140 and 156 Iris Hardwick Library of Photographs for the picture on page 8 and the back of the book jacket. Roger and Tessa Adamson for their assistance with certain Greek information, the staff of the Exeter Library for their patience, and Rowena Stott for her continuing interest.

Index